McGraw-Hill Reading

Wonders

Your Turn
Practice Book

McGraw Hill **Education**

Bothell, WA • Chicago, IL • Columbus, OH • New York, NY

www.mheonline.com/readingwonders

Send all inquiries to:
McGraw-Hill Education
2 Penn Plaza
New York, NY 10121

Printed in the United States of America.

14 15 16 17 18 19 LHS 20 19 18

Contents

Unit 1 • Growing and Learning

Contents

Unit 2 • Figure It Out

Contents

Unit 3 • One of a Kind

Be Unique

Leadership

Discoveries

New Ideas

TIME For Kids

Contents

Unit 4 • Meet the Challenge

Contents

Unit 5 • Take Action

Contents

Unit 6 • Think It Over

Name _____

educated	inspired	ached	discovery
satisfied	concentrate	improved	effort

Use a word from the box to answer each question. Then use the word in a sentence.

1. What can you become if you study often? _____

   _____

2. What is another word for *hurt*? _____

   _____

3. What word might describe someone who is pleased after a meal?

   _____

4. What is another word for *hard work*? _____

   _____

5. If someone caused others to take action, what did they do?

   _____

6. What word means the same thing as *finding for the first time*?

   _____

7. If you want to carefully study for a test, what do you need to do?

   _____

8. What is another word for *got better*? _____

   _____

Name _____

Read the selection. Complete the character graphic organizer.

Character	
Wants or Needs	**Feelings**
Actions	**Traits**

Name _____

Read the passage. Use the visualize strategy to help form pictures in your mind.

River Rescue

	Enid lived in the jungle with her family and friends. Her home
12	had tall green trees, cool blue streams, and bright and beautiful
23	flowers. It had enough tasty, fresh fruit to last forever.
33	The only thing Enid loved and adored more than her jungle
44	home was reading. She read stories about fish. She read stories
55	about dogs. She read stories about castles in France. Sometimes
65	her friends told her that she read too much.
74	"Enid! You always have your trunk in a book! Your eyes will
86	start to ache if you read too much," her friend Mabel would say.
99	"Come swimming instead."
102	"I'll swim later. I'm reading about a girl with ruby red
113	slippers."
114	Every evening after dinner, Enid would try to read her favorite
125	stories to her friends. They would listen for a little while, but one of
139	them would always say, "Hearing stories isn't fun! Let's go play!"
150	Enid kept reading. She hoped she would inspire her friends to
161	read.
162	One day, after a heavy rain, Enid was trying to read a story
175	about a beaver building a dam. In the middle of chapter 12, she
188	heard a cry for help.
193	Books are a good way to become educated. However, even
203	Enid would put a book down if someone needed her help.
214	"Help!" said the small, meek voice. It came from the river's edge.
226	"I know that voice!" said Enid. "It's my friend Mabel!"

Name _____

Enid ran toward Mabel's voice. When she reached the river's edge she was surprised and shocked by what she saw. The usually calm, flat, clear water was now dark and swirling with splashing white waves. On the other shore on the opposite side of the river was tiny Mabel.

"Enid. What can we do?" asked her friend Harold. "We were about to play in the river like we always do. Mabel was on the other side of the river about to pick some fruit for lunch. Then it happened! The river got deeper and wider all of a sudden. It was magic."

"It wasn't magic," said Enid. "It is a flood. I read about it. Sometimes when it rains too much like it did today, rivers can swell and get bigger without a warning."

"What can we do to help Mabel?" asked Harold. "Did you also read about something to help when rivers get too big?"

Enid thought about her book about the beaver's dam. "Yes! We can build a dam. A dam is like a wall in the river. It slows down the water. When it slows down, Mabel can cross back to us safely."

"How do we make a dam?" asked Harold.

"Like this," said Enid. She rolled round, gray stones toward the river, slowly building a wall in the water. Her friends began helping her, assisting Enid in building the dam. Soon, it was complete and the water slowed. Mabel was able to cross back.

After that day, Enid's friends were satisfied to read books with her and listen to her stories.

Name _____

A. Reread the passage and answer the questions.

1. What do Enid's actions in the first half of the story tell you about her?

_____

_____

_____

2. Why do you think Enid wants her friends to read and listen to stories?

_____

_____

_____

3. A character's actions make the events in a story happen. If Enid did not like reading, how would the story be different?

_____

_____

_____

B. Work with a partner. Read the passage aloud. Pay attention to expression. Stop after one minute. Fill out the chart.

	Words Read	–	Number of Errors	=	Words Correct Score
First Read		–		=	
Second Read		–		=	

Name _____

The Bookworm's Big Surprise

"You're not really a bookworm," the caterpillars called to the bookworm. "You're a caterpillar like us! Come with us. It's time for us to go spin our cocoons! We're going to turn into butterflies."

Shocked, the bookworm said, "I want to stay and munch on my books."

"Butterflies can munch on books too!" the caterpillars said. "You don't have to be a bookworm to like books!"

Answer the questions about the text.

1. How do you know this text is a fantasy?

_____

_____

2. Why does the bookworm at first not want to change?

_____

_____

3. What is the lesson of this text?

_____

4. A fantasy may have an illustration. How might an illustration show that this text is a fantasy?

_____

_____

Name _____

**Read each passage. Underline the synonym that means about
the same thing as each word in bold. Then write the meaning of
the word in bold on the line.**

1. I was excited to go to the country and pick apples with my family. I have
   always **adored** making pies and muffins with fresh apples. It turns out my
   sister is crazy about apples, too. She picked twice as many apples as I did!

   _____

   _____

2. When people first meet me, they think that I am **meek**. However, they soon
   change their minds. When I start telling jokes and stories they laugh. Then
   they see that I'm really not the quiet person they thought I was.

   _____

   _____

3. Our class was **shocked** when we walked into the room on Friday. Our
   teacher was throwing us a party! Nobody even knew about it. Even though
   we were all stunned, we all sure had a lot of fun.

   _____

   _____

4. My family says that I am just the **opposite** of my sister. My favorite subject
   is art. Her favorite subject is math. She wants to have a cat for a pet. I want
   to find the perfect dog. We may be completely different from each other,
   but we are still best friends.

   _____

   _____

Name _____

A. Circle the word that has a short *a* or a short *i* vowel sound. Then write it on the line to complete the sentence.

1. I need a _____ for my letter.

   box   stamp   pen

2. We saw the man _____ his bus.

   drive   miss   get

3. How far can you _____ the ball?

   kick   throw   take

4. The _____ will march in the parade.

   mayor   team   band

B. Words in the same word family have a common spelling pattern. Sort the words in the box by placing them in the correct word family.

glad	click	spill	stand	bill	hand
camp	ramp	mad	pink	stick	think

1. *-ill*   3. *-amp*   5. *-ad*

   _____   _____   _____

   _____   _____   _____

2. *-and*   4. *-ink*   6. *-ick*

   _____   _____   _____

   _____   _____   _____

Name _____

Evidence is details and examples from a text that support a writer's opinion. This student wrote his or her opinion on whether or not the author gave enough information to reveal that it was Enid's love of reading that made the story events happen.

Topic sentence → In "River Rescue," I think the author does a good job showing how Enid's love of reading saves the day.

Evidence → In the story, the author says that Enid loves to read. Her friend, Mabel, would rather play. Mabel does not think reading is important. One day, Mabel gets trapped in a flood. Enid reads how to help in a book. She is the only one who knows what to do. Enid is a hero!

Concluding statement → hero! The author shows that because of Enid's love of reading she was about to save her friend.

Write a paragraph about a story you read. Find text evidence to support your opinion of how the author uses the character's actions and feelings to make story events happen.

Write a topic sentence: _____

_____

Cite evidence from the text: _____

_____

_____

_____

End with a concluding statement: _____

_____

Name _____

A. Read the draft model. Use the questions that follow the draft to help you think about how you can focus on a central event.

Draft Model

Polly Pig always played in the mud. It was warm out. The mud felt good to her. She saw another animal in the mud.

---

1. When exactly was Polly Pig playing in the mud?

2. What details would tell how warm it was then?

3. What details would tell how the mud felt?

4. What kind of animal did Polly Pig see?

B. Now revise the draft by focusing on a central event and adding details that will help readers learn more about what happened to Polly Pig.

_____

_____

_____

_____

_____

_____

Name _____

| celebrate | pride | disappointment | remind |
| precious | tradition | courage | symbols |

Finish each sentence using the vocabulary word provided.

1. **(tradition)** Our family gets together for _____

_____ .

2. **(celebrate)** After the girl won the spelling contest, _____

_____ .

3. **(courage)** He won a badge of honor _____

_____ .

4. **(disappointment)** When I didn't get to see my friend, _____

_____ .

5. **(symbols)** Shaking hands and hugging are _____

_____ .

6. **(pride)** My mom was so happy for me _____

_____ .

7. **(remind)** I always forget my lunch _____

_____ .

8. **(precious)** This photo of my grandfather _____

_____ .

Name _____

Read the selection. Complete the sequence graphic organizer.

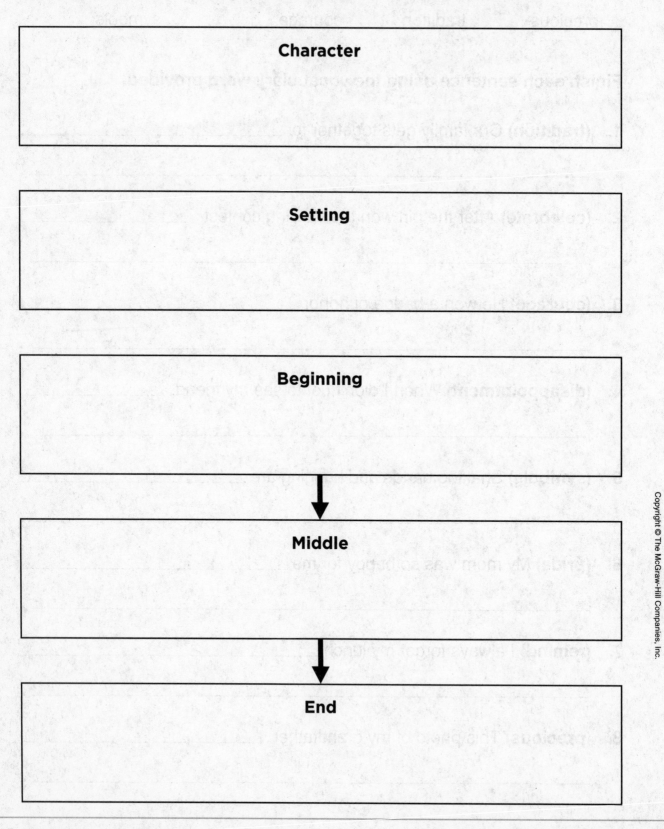

Character

Setting

Beginning

Middle

End

Name _____

Read the passage. Use the visualize strategy to help you understand what the characters are describing.

Giving Thanks

10	Tom was happy because it was the last day before Thanksgiving weekend. He grabbed his lunch from his kitchen
19	table and went to school. In the lunchroom after morning classes,
30	he sat next to Ana, a new student from India. He had never talked
44	to her before.
47	"Are you excited for the long weekend?" he asked.
56	"Of course," she said. "But why do we have these days off?"
68	"Thanksgiving, of course!" Tom said. "Do you know what it is?"
79	"No, we don't have it where I am from," she said.

Thanksgiving in America — 90

93	"Oh, Thanksgiving is so much fun," Tom said. "We get to
104	spend precious time with family and friends. First, we have a big
116	feast with turkey, mashed potatoes, and pie. After the feast, I go
128	outside and play football with my brothers."
135	"But why do you have this tradition?" she asked.
144	"It's to remind everyone to give thanks for our food and
155	everything from the past year," he said. "I learned in Ms. Boone's
167	class that the first Thanksgiving was way back in 1621 between
178	the English Colonists and Native Americans."

Name _____

Thanksgiving in India

"Wow, that sounds great," said Ana. "In my country we also give thanks. We do it in a different way."

"Really?" Tom said. "How?"

"I am from a place in India called Tamil Nadu," she said. "In January, we celebrate something called Pongal."

"Pongal? What does that mean?" Tom asked.

"It's an Indian dish," she said. "During the Pongal festival, food is cooked in pots until it boils and spills over. It is a symbol of good times for us."

"Wow," Tom said. "How do you celebrate?"

"First, we give thanks to the rain and sun for help with farming. We even thank the cattle," said Ana. "Then we throw away old things and wear new clothes. We eat food and spend time with family."

Sharing traditions

"I thought that the United States was the only country that had a holiday like Thanksgiving," Tom said. "I guess I was wrong."

"Yes, there are many types of harvest festivals all over the world where people give thanks for food and crops," she said.

"I guess we all have a lot to be thankful for," he said, and they both agreed.

Name _____

A. Reread the passage and answer the questions.

1. In paragraph six, what is the first thing that Tom does on Thanksgiving?

_____

_____

2. What is the next thing that Tom does on Thanksgiving?

_____

_____

3. In the passage, find another example of sequence under the head Thanksgiving in India. What is the first thing that happens in this example?

_____

_____

B. Work with a partner. Read the passage aloud. Pay attention to phrasing. Stop after one minute. Fill out the chart.

	Words Read	–	Number of Errors	=	Words Correct Score
First Read		–		=	
Second Read		–		=	

Name _____

A Family Tradition

My mother asked, "How do you say good-bye to your lola, Jomar?" *Lola* is the Filipino word for "grandmother."

"Please remind me," I said.

"In the Philippines," my mother explained, "we have a tradition called *Mano Po*. When you say 'hello' or 'good-bye' to your elders, you touch their right hand to your forehead. It is a sign of respect."

I touched my lola's hand to my forehead. "*Mano Po*, Lola!" I said.

Answer the questions about the text.

1. How do you know this text is realistic fiction?

_____

_____

2. What is dialogue? How does it show that the text is realistic?

_____

_____

3. What is an example of actual words the characters speak?

_____

_____

4. What does the illustration add to the text?

_____

Name _____

Read each sentence below. Underline the context clues that help you understand the meaning of each word in bold. Then write the word's meaning on the line.

1. He **grabbed** his lunch from his kitchen table and went to school.

_____

2. "We get to **spend** precious time with family and friends."

_____

3. "First, we have a big **feast** with turkey, mashed potatoes, and pie."

_____

4. "During the Pongal festival, food is cooked in pots until it **boils** and spills over."

_____

5. "Yes, there are many **types** of harvest festivals all over the world where people give thanks for food and crops," she said.

_____

6. "Yes, there are many types of **harvest** festivals all over the world where people give thanks for food and crops," she said.

_____

Name _____

A. Circle the word with the correct short vowel sound to complete each sentence.

1. I like to _____ down the hill when it snows.

   short e   slide   sled   run

2. Did you find your missing _____?

   short o   sock   coat   cup

3. He runs and _____ when he plays basketball.

   short u   leaps   shoots   jumps

4. The farmer planted the _____ in April.

   short o   corn   crops   oats

5. Everyone helped clean the _____ in the city park.

   short e   mess   stream   seats

B. Write the correct *-s, -ed,* and *-ing* forms to complete each set.

	+ s	**+ ed**	**+ ing**
1. tap	_____	tapped	_____
2. stop	stops	_____	_____
3. clap	_____	_____	clapping
4. step	_____	stepped	_____
5. skip	_____	_____	_____

Name _____

> *Evidence* is details and examples from a text that support a writer's ideas. This student wrote about how the author uses what Tom and Ana do and say to create the plot, or events, in the story.
>
> **Topic sentence** →   In "Giving Thanks," the author uses what Tom and Ana do and say to create the plot of the story.
>
> **Evidence** → At the beginning, Tom asks Ana if she knows what Thanksgiving is. When Ana says no, he tells her all about his Thanksgiving. Then, in the middle of the story, Ana talks about one of her family's traditions. At the end both agree that being thankful can mean celebrating in different ways. The author created
>
> **Concluding statement** → a beginning, middle, and end of the story by using what Tom and Ana said and did.

Write a paragraph about a story you read. Find text evidence to show how the author uses what the characters say and do to create the plot, or events, in the story. Use text evidence to support your ideas.

Write a topic sentence: _____

_____

Cite evidence from the text: _____

_____

_____

_____

End with a concluding statement: _____

_____

Name _____

A. Read the draft model. Use the questions that follow the draft to help you think about what descriptive details you can add.

Draft Model

We make dinner for the New Year. Every person gets to make something for the meal. We all help each other. Then we wait until midnight to begin our big family dinner.

---

1. Who is making the dinner?

2. What descriptive details would help the reader visualize the people in the story?

3. In what ways do the people help each other?

4. What descriptive details could provide more information about the dinner?

B. Now revise the draft by adding descriptive details that help the readers learn more about the people making dinner.

_____

_____

_____

_____

_____

_____

Name _____

| admires | community | practicing | scared |
| classmate | contribute | pronounce | tumbled |

Use a word from the box to answer each question. Then use the word in a sentence.

1. What is another word for *afraid*? _____

_____

2. What word can describe a friend who sits next to you at school?

_____

3. What is another word for *give*? _____

_____

4. What helps people get better at doing something? _____

_____

5. What word means *say the sound of*? _____

_____

6. What word describes a place where people live and work together?

_____

7. What word means *thinks well of*? _____

_____

8. What happened to the fruit when it fell out and rolled to the ground?

_____

Name _____

Read the selection. Complete the sequence graphic organizer.

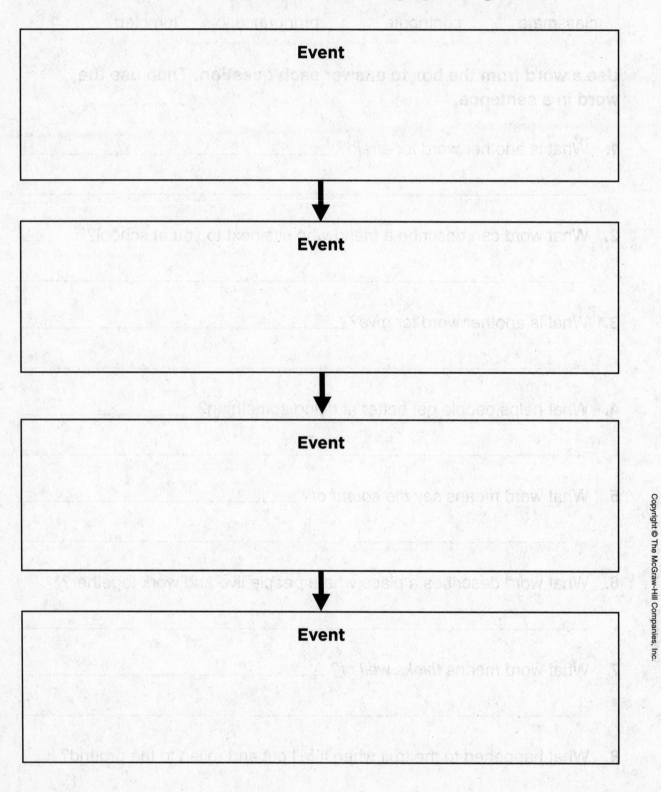

Name _____

Read the passage. Use the ask and answer questions strategy to be sure you understand what you read.

Joseph Bruchac

Growing Up Near Mountains

4	Joseph Bruchac grew up in the mountains of New York. He
15	lived with his grandmother and grandfather. Young Joseph loved
24	to go with his grandfather everywhere he went. His grandfather
34	showed him how to walk softly through the woods and how to
46	fish in the lakes and rivers.
52	As a child, Joseph spent time working in his grandparents'
62	store. When he made mistakes, his grandfather would never shout
72	or yell at him. Instead, he would talk to Joseph about what had
85	happened. That way Joseph could know how to do better the next
97	time. During the winter, farmers would come to the store. They
108	would sit around the stove and tell Joseph stories.
117	While growing up, Joseph loved to read and write. Joseph's
127	grandmother kept bookshelves in the house full of books. There
137	was always plenty to read. He liked to read storybooks about
148	animals. He also liked reading poetry. He even wrote some
158	poems of his own! One time, he wrote a poem for his teacher.
171	She was very proud.

Name _____

Abenaki Storyteller

Joseph's grandfather was an Abenaki Native American. Joseph became interested in stories told by the Abenaki. When he was in college, Joseph would sometimes visit Native American elders. He would listen to them tell stories. These stories were fun to listen to. But they also taught great lessons about life. Later, Joseph started to have children of his own. He wrote down the stories he heard. Then he read them to his two sons. Soon after that, Joseph began to write children's books. These books told the stories of the Abenaki and other Native American peoples.

Helping Others

In the fourth grade, Joseph's teacher told him, "Whatever you want to do, you should do it." Joseph wanted to write and help others. And that's just what he did. First, he began to write stories. These stories taught children about being kind. They also taught children to care for the Earth. Then, Joseph went to schools all over the United States. He read his stories to children. Now, Joseph helps other writers share their stories.

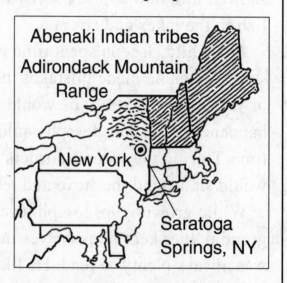

Map of Joseph Bruchac's homeland

Today, Joseph spends time in his garden. He has gardens all around his house. The inside of his house is full of many plants. Joseph has been all over the world. But he still lives in the hometown where he grew up. "It is a place I love," says Joseph. He still likes to walk through the woods and mountains. Every day he gets ideas for brand-new stories.

Name _____

A. Reread the passage and answer the questions.

1. What happened during the winter at Joseph's grandparents' store?

_____

_____

2. What happened next after Joseph read stories to his sons?

_____

_____

3. Reread the fifth paragraph. What did Joseph do after he began to write stories?

_____

_____

B. Work with a partner. Read the passage aloud. Pay attention to rate. Stop after one minute. Fill out the chart.

	Words Read	–	Number of Errors	=	Words Correct Score
First Read		–		=	
Second Read		–		=	

Name _____

Keith Little

During World War II, I was a soldier and fought battles in the Marshall Islands and on Iwo Jima in the Pacific Ocean. I was one of the Navajo code talkers. The code talkers used the language of the Navajo people to send messages to the troops. The enemy didn't know this language and couldn't read our code. Our work helped the United States win many battles. After the war, I taught people about Navajo language and culture.

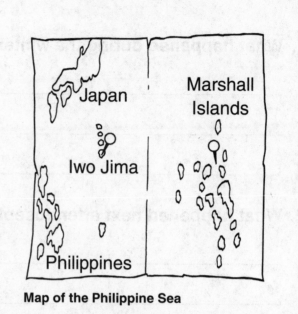

Map of the Philippine Sea

Answer the questions about the text.

1. How do you know this text is an autobiography?

_____

_____

2. What text features does the text include?

_____

3. What information does the map give you?

_____

_____

Name _____

Underline the compound word in each sentence. Then write its definition. Use a dictionary to help you.

1. His grandfather showed him how to walk softly through the woods.

_____

_____

2. He liked to read storybooks about animals.

_____

_____

3. There were plenty of bookshelves in the house full of books.

_____

_____

4. But he still lives in the hometown where he grew up.

_____

_____

Name _____

A. Read each sentence. Underline the word that has a long vowel sound and a final e.

1. Each summer they camp at the lake.

2. The plane should land at noon today.

3. The boy read about the life of his hero.

4. Our teacher pointed to each continent on the globe.

5. The woman plans to skate on the pond this winter.

B. Circle the word with the correct -ed or -ing spelling to complete each sentence. Then write it on the line.

1. I am _____ my money to spend on vacation.
      saveing   saving

2. He _____ the broccoli and liked it.
      tasted   tasteed

3. We are _____ plans to visit our grandparents.
      making   makeing

4. The teacher _____ the spelling tests last night.
      gradeed   graded

5. I have been _____ ever since I heard the good news.
      smilling   smiling

6. The artist _____ the clay into a small bowl.
      shaped   shapped

Name _____

Evidence is details and examples from a text that support a writer's ideas. This student wrote about how the author uses signal words to show the sequence of important events in a text.

Topic sentence →   In "Joseph Bruchac," the author tells the events of Joseph's life in order. First I read about what he liked to do when he was young. Joseph loved to read

Evidence → and spend time with his grandfather. Then I read how Joseph listened to stories and then wrote them down. He wrote books for children! At the end, I learned what Joseph is doing now. The author tells

Concluding statement → Joseph's life in order and it helps me understand how he became a famous writer and storyteller.

Write a paragraph about a story you read. Find text evidence to show how the author uses signal words to put important events in time order. Use text evidence to support your ideas.

Write a topic sentence: _____

_____

Cite evidence from the text: _____

_____

_____

_____

End with a concluding statement: _____

_____

Name _____

A. Read the draft model. Use the questions that follow the draft to help you think about how you can add language to show the time and order of events.

Draft Model

I went camping with my dad. I helped my dad put up our tent. We built a fire. We roasted hot dogs and marshmallows. We put out the fire and went to sleep in our tent.

---

1. When did the writer go camping?

2. What did the writer do first?

3. What word or words that show order would tell when the writer roasted marshmallows?

4. What words would help signal what the writer did last?

B. Now revise the draft by adding words that show time and order to help readers learn more about how the camping trip unfolded.

_____

_____

_____

_____

_____

Name _____

design	simple	investigation	encouraged
substitutes	quality	examine	solution

Use a word from the box to answer each question. Then use the word in a sentence.

1. What is another word for *a careful search for something*?

_____

2. How might you describe a product that is well made? _____

_____

3. What word might describe an answer to a problem? _____

_____

4. What would you be doing if you were to create a plan? _____

_____

5. When you inspect something closely, what do you do? _____

_____

6. What is another word for *given hope to do something*? _____

_____

7. What do you call things that take the place of other things?

_____

8. What is another word for *easy*? _____

_____

Name _____

Read the selection. Complete the cause and effect graphic organizer.

Cause		Effect
First	→	
Next	→	
Then	→	
Finally	→	

Name _____

Read the passage. Use the ask and answer questions strategy to be sure you understand what you read.

Victor Ochoa's New Idea

11	Have you ever made something that no one else had made
24	before? It is not an easy thing to do. People who make something
35	new are called inventors. They look around and see what can
48	be made better and then they do it! Victor Ochoa was one of
60	those people. He made many things. One of them was a flying
72	machine. Victor looked at birds to get his ideas. He wanted to
	learn everything about how birds flew.

78	**Many Jobs**
80	Victor was born in Mexico in 1850 and grew up in Texas. He
93	lived all over the United States. He loved to work with writers.
105	He wrote for newspapers. He even started two new papers. He
116	worked hard and never gave up, no matter how hard the job was.

129	**A New Plane**
132	Victor's mind was a motor that never turned off. He was
143	always thinking of new ways to make life better. In 1908, he was
156	thinking about the way that birds fly. He thought that he could
168	make a plane that flew like a bird. So he set to work.

Name _____

The center of the plane was made of two bikes set next to each other. It looked a little like a car. It had a small motor that sat between the two bikes. The back was shaped like a bird's tail. The wings were made of canvas and steel pipes. What made this plane different was that the wings could be folded down just like a bird's wings. This was so it could be put in a small shed or barn. This way, everyone could keep a plane at a house or on a farm.

Victor started a company that would make this new plane. He asked the Navy to use his new plane. He wrote the Navy a letter telling them why he thought his plane would be just what they needed. He worked very hard to make his plane work. He worked on it for over twenty years. No one knows if it ever flew.

Other New Ideas

Victor did not let this problem keep him from making other things. Making new things from new ideas was the blood in his veins. He made a new pen that

Victor Ochoa's plane was made of two bikes.

held its own ink. Another thing he came up with was a motor that worked both forward and backward.

Never Give Up

Victor was a spinning top. He was always making new things. He wanted to help other people with his ideas. Not all of his ideas worked. No one who tries something new is successful every time, though. The important part is to keep trying. Victor Ochoa was someone who never stopped trying.

Name _____

A. Reread the passage and answer the questions.

1. What was the cause of Victor's actions in the third paragraph?

_____

_____

_____

2. What effect did this cause have on Victor?

_____

_____

_____

3. What kinds of things did Victor invent to make life better?

_____

_____

_____

B. Work with a partner. Read the passage aloud. Pay attention to expression. Stop after one minute. Fill out the chart.

	Words Read	–	Number of Errors	=	Words Correct Score
First Read		–		=	
Second Read		–		=	

Name _____

George Crum's Potato Chip

George Crum was born in 1822. Later on in life, he became the chef at Moon's Lake House in Saratoga, New York. One day in 1853, a customer ordered french-fried potatoes but sent them back to the kitchen. He said they were too thick and soft. Annoyed, Crum sliced some potatoes very thin and fried them crispy. They were great! George Crum had invented the potato chip.

Thinly slice potato

Brush with butter on tray

Bake at 500° F for 20 minutes

Answer the questions about the text.

1. **How do you know this text is a biography?**

   _____

2. **What text feature does this text include?**

   _____

3. **What does the diagram show you? What title would you give this diagram?**

   _____

4. **How can you tell that the events in the text are in the order that they happened?**

   _____

Name _____

A. Read each sentence from the passage. Then write what two things are being compared in the metaphor on the lines.

1. Victor's mind was a motor that never turned off.

_____

_____

2. Making new things from new ideas was the blood in his veins.

_____

_____

3. Victor was a spinning top.

_____

_____

B. Reread the passage. Use what you have learned to write two metaphors based on the life of Victor Ochoa.

1. _____

_____

2. _____

_____

Name _____

A. Read each sentence. Circle the word that has a long *a* sound spelled *ai*, *ay*, or *eigh*. Write the word on the line and underline the long *a* spelling.

1. The snail left a slimy path across the sidewalk. _____

2. The wind caused the trees to sway wildly. _____

3. The farmer planted the grain to grow wheat. _____

4. Please weigh the apples because we need two pounds. _____

5. My new winter coat is gray and blue. _____

B. Read each sentence and circle the plural nouns. Underline the -*s* or -*es* ending in each plural word.

1. The girls found many seashells on the beach.

2. The artist bought new oils and paintbrushes.

3. The boys helped me stack the boxes.

4. I wrote the addresses on each of the pages.

5. She won free passes to all the games.

6. The camels have long eyelashes.

Name _____

> *Evidence* is details and examples from a text that support a writer's ideas. This student wrote about how the author uses text features.
>
> **Topic sentence** →   In "Victor Ochoa's New Idea," the author uses text features to help readers understand the topic better. Headings tell me how the information is organized.
>
> **Evidence** → For example, the heading "Many Jobs" tells about some of the jobs Victor had. It organizes the information about his life. The picture of Victor's plane and its caption give extra information that
>
> **Concluding statement** → is not in the text. In this selection, the author uses text features to organize and give more information about the topic.

Write a paragraph about a story you read. Find text evidence to show how the author uses text features. Use text evidence to support your ideas.

Write a topic sentence: _____

_____

Cite evidence from the text: _____

_____

_____

_____

End with a concluding statement: _____

_____

Name _____

A. Read the draft model. Use the questions that follow the draft to help you think about how you can use time-order words and phrases in your writing.

Draft Model

Benjamin Franklin was a great inventor. One important invention of his was the lightning rod. He invented bifocal glasses to help people see.

---

1. What was the first invention that Franklin created?

2. What time-order words and phrases would help put the events of Franklin's life in order?

3. What was the later invention that Franklin created?

B. Now revise the draft by adding time-order words and phrases to help readers follow events.

_____

_____

_____

_____

_____

_____

_____

Name _____

| national | grand | carved | clues |
| landmark | massive | monument | traces |

Use the context clues in each sentence to help you decide which vocabulary word fits best in the blank.

The art museum was one of Phoebe's favorite places to visit. It was a _____ and an important historical site. In fact, it housed so many great works of art it was considered a _____ treasure by most people. Each time she visited this museum, she smiled. There was always a _____ adventure or story around every corner.

Phoebe loved to visit the sculpture garden. There were dolphins, people, and other creatures _____ out of stone and marble. It impressed her that someone could carefully cut such shapes out of rock.

She loved to see new paintings on display. Some were no bigger than her notebook. However, some were so _____ that she wondered how one person could have painted them!

Today, Phoebe was eager to see a _____ that was on loan from another museum. The memorial was over three hundred years old and had been found in Italy. Historians felt that the piece provided _____ about a little-known artist. It also told a story about life in a small Italian village hundreds of years ago.

As she walked to the exhibit, Phoebe wondered if years from now someone would be looking at one of her own paintings to find _____ or evidence about what life used to be like. The thought made her want to create a new painting when she returned home!

Name _____

Read the selection. Complete the main idea and details graphic organizer.

Main Idea
Detail
Detail
Detail

Name _____

Read the passage. Use the ask and answer questions strategy to tell about the most important details of the passage.

Building a Landmark

	Have you ever made a sand castle? Maybe you've built
10	something in the snow or dirt. Have you thought that something
21	you made on land would last for a long time, though? In Ohio
34	there are Native American mounds on the land. These mounds
44	have been there for thousands of years. The Ohio mounds act as
56	landmarks, or important sites. They also help us understand our
66	country's history.
68	Native American tribes created Ohio's mounds. Today, there
76	are over 70 mounds left. People visit them each year. One of
88	these mounds is called Serpent Mound. It is 1,370 feet long. The
100	mound looks like a big snake. This is the world's longest burial
112	mound! Objects from other tribes are in Serpent Mound. This
122	makes researchers think that many tribes made the mound. A lot
133	of tribes might have made this one mound to share.
143	The mounds are different shapes. Miamisburg Mound is
151	shaped like a cone. It is the largest cone mound in Ohio. It is
165	believed that the Adena tribe made this mound. There are 116
176	steps. Visitors can climb them to the top.

Name _____

How did the tribes make these mounds? At Fort Ancient Mounds, people used clam shells to dig the dirt. They also used sticks. They carried the dirt for the mounds in baskets. The baskets weighed about 40 pounds. Do you know why a tribe would want to build these mounds? Some people say they were used as a calendar. The mounds have walls that total 18,000 feet in length. This means carrying dirt to build them was a lot of hard work.

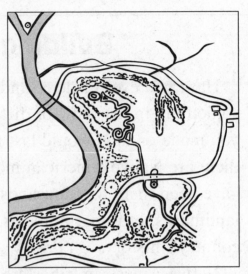

Map of Serpent Mound Park, Adams County, Ohio

The Newark Earthworks are geometric mounds. They are the world's largest set like this. Researchers think these mounds were used to study stars. They might have been used for gatherings, too.

Cultures leave behind stories. Some stories are in books. Some are in artwork. In Ohio, Native American tribes left behind mounds. Not all questions about the mounds have been answered. But these landmarks have still helped us learn more of our country's history.

Social and Sacred Places

Some researchers think that the Ohio River Valley mounds were used for social reasons. Others think they were for ceremonial reasons. Today, you can visit them. Maybe you can come up with your own answer of how the mounds were used.

Name _____

A. Reread the passage and answer the questions.

1. What are three key details in paragraph 4?

_____

_____

_____

2. How are these details connected?

_____

_____

3. What is the main idea of the whole passage?

_____

_____

B. Work with a partner. Read the passage aloud. Pay attention to accuracy and phrasing. Stop after one minute. Fill out the chart.

	Words Read	–	Number of Errors	=	Words Correct Score
First Read		–		=	
Second Read		–		=	

Name _____

The Lincoln Memorial

The architect Henry Bacon had a very specific idea of what he wanted when he designed the Lincoln Memorial. He had studied architecture in Europe and was very impressed with the buildings of ancient Greece. He wanted his memorial to remind people of the city of Athens in Greece, the birthplace of democracy. That way, people who saw the memorial would remember the ancient tradition of democracy that Abraham Lincoln fought to keep alive.

The Gettysburg Address is...

- a speech given by Abraham Lincoln on November 19, 1863, during the Civil War.
- written on the south wall of the Lincoln Memorial.
- dedicated to the soldiers who fought and died at the Battle of Gettysburg, so "that government of the people, by the people, and for the people, shall not perish from the earth."

Answer the questions about the text.

1. **How can you tell that this is informational text?**

_____

_____

2. **What text feature is included? How does it relate to the main topic?**

_____

_____

3. **What did Henry Bacon want the Lincoln Memorial to remind people of?**

_____

_____

Name _____

Read each sentence. Underline the context clues that help you figure out the meaning of each word in bold. Then write the meaning of the word on the line. Use a dictionary to help you.

1. Today, there are over 70 Native American mounds **left**.

   _____

2. When you get to the corner you should turn **left**.

   _____

3. At Fort Ancient Mounds, people used clam shells to dig the dirt. They also used **sticks**.

   _____

4. When you add glue to the paper it **sticks** to any surface.

   _____

5. Cultures leave behind **stories**. Some stories are in books.

   _____

6. This building has four **stories** and I live on the third level.

   _____

Name _____

A. Read each sentence. Circle the word that has the long o sound and underline the long o spelling. Write the word on the line.

1. What time will you be home? _____

2. It is too cold to play outside. _____

3. My aunt lives near the coast in California. _____

4. Can you show me how to do this math problem? _____

5. I hurt my toe playing soccer. _____

B. Use the words from the box to make the best compound word. Write the compound word on the line.

time	bowl	book
crow	boat	made

1. home + _____ = _____

2. fish + _____ = _____

3. over + _____ = _____

4. motor + _____ = _____

5. note + _____ = _____

6. scare + _____ = _____

Name _____

Evidence is details and examples from a text that support a writer's ideas. This student found evidence that compares how two authors present important information and key details about the same topic.

Topic sentence → The author of "Building a Landmark" and the author of "The Lincoln Memorial" give information and key details about landmarks. Both authors focus

Evidence → on landmarks. The author of "Building a Landmark" tells about how early peoples created and used their own landmarks. The author of "The Lincoln Memorial" tells how the Lincoln Memorial was created. The Lincoln Memorial is a more modern landmark and was created to help people remember

Concluding statement → an event in history. Both authors present important information and key details about how landmarks were created and used.

Write about two texts that tell about the same topic. Use text evidence to compare how the authors present important information and key details.

Write a topic sentence: _____

_____

Cite evidence from the text: _____

_____

_____

End with a concluding statement: _____

_____

Name _____

A. Read the draft model. Use the questions that follow the draft to help you think about using different sentence types.

Draft Model

Parks are important because they offer a place to experience nature. Parks are places to have picnics, play sports, and do many other activities. In cities, a park can be a good place to get away from the commotion.

---

1. What type of sentence is included in the model?

2. How does the writer's chosen sentence type affect the way you read the model?

3. What different sentence types can be added to the model?

4. How would adding different sentence types change the way you read the model?

B. Now revise the draft by using different sentence types to make the writing more interesting.

_____

_____

_____

_____

_____

Name _____

created   interfere   timid   awkward

furiously   attempt   cooperation   involved

Finish each sentence using the vocabulary word provided.

1. (awkward) The chair has one leg that is shorter than the others,

_____ .

2. (timid) He had not met many new people, _____

_____ .

3. (created) My sister and I _____

_____ .

4. (furiously) The energetic dog _____

_____ .

5. (interfere) I was annoyed _____

_____ .

6. (involved) We can become _____

_____ .

7. (attempt) I sat down with my mom _____

_____ .

8. (cooperation) Chores go more quickly _____

_____ .

Name _____

Read the selection. Complete the theme graphic organizer.

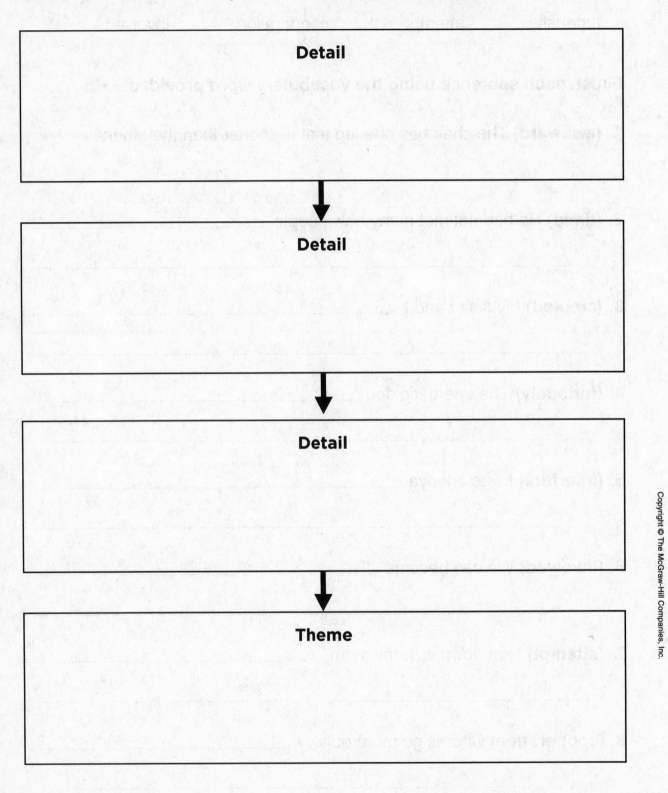

Name _____

Read the passage. Use the make, confirm, and revise predictions strategy to predict what will happen in the story.

Why People and Birds Are Friends

	A long time ago, people of the world were far apart. It was
13	easier to get lost then. People and animals did not talk to each
26	other. It was easier that way. But things change.
35	Jungles are enormous. It is easy to lose your way and feel
47	tiny. This is what happened to two brothers on a hunting trip.
59	They planned to be gone for two days. But five days later, they
72	were lost. They were farther from home than they had ever been.
84	Every day they would walk in one direction. They thought it
95	would take them home. Every day they would stop when it got
107	dark. But they would be no closer to being found by anyone.
119	Luckily, they knew how to camp. They also knew how to find
131	food and firewood. The older brother went to find firewood, and
142	the younger brother went to gather food and water. He looked
153	for more than an hour. But he could not find anything to feed his
167	brother and himself. He was very tired, so he sat down to rest.
180	The young boy sat, listening to the warm wind in the leaves.
192	He noticed a bird in the tree above him. He watched as it jumped
206	about. Then he heard a voice.
212	"I know where your parents are! I know where your parents
223	are!"

Name _____

The boy looked around to see who was talking to him. He didn't see anyone. He was confused. He heard the words again. In a moment, he understood that the bird was talking to him!

The young boy stared at the bird for a minute. Then he said, "Can you really help my brother and me get home?"

The bird hopped from one branch to the next. She said, "Yes, I can. I know the village you live in. I can take you back there. I only ask for something in return: I require three insects to eat. That will make me strong enough to guide you home."

The young boy quickly agreed to feed the bird. He ran back to his camp as fast as he could. He found his brother sitting in front of the fire. He told his brother about the bird. His brother did not believe him at first. But finally he slowly agreed to go with the boy to meet the talking bird.

When they found the bird again, it repeated the offer to the older boy. He also immediately agreed. The boys went to find insects for the bird. It waited patiently on a tree branch. They found several insects. The bird chose a few and gulped them down, one, two, three! "We leave in the morning," she said.

The next morning, the boys followed the bird home. It took several days. The bird always waited for the boys to catch up before flying ahead. When they finally got home, the boys' parents were very happy to see them. The family promised that they and their children's children would always feed hungry birds. That is why birds sing to humans, and humans feed birds.

Name _____

A. Reread the passage and answer the questions.

1. Why does the younger brother in the story need help?

_____

_____

_____

2. What does the bird ask for in return for her help?

_____

_____

_____

3. What is the theme of this story?

_____

_____

B. Work with a partner. Read the passage aloud. Pay attention to intonation and phrasing. Stop after one minute. Fill out the chart.

	Words Read	–	Number of Errors	=	Words Correct Score
First Read		–		=	
Second Read		–		=	

Name _____

The Ant and the Dove

One day, an ant was drinking water from a stream. Suddenly, he slipped and fell into the water. A dove was sitting in a nearby tree and saw the ant drowning. She pulled a leaf from the tree and dropped it into the water. The ant climbed onto the leaf and floated to the shore.

The next day, the ant saw a hunter sneaking up behind the dove with a net. The dove did not see the hunter. The ant crept up and bit the hunter on the foot. The hunter shouted in pain and dropped his net. The dove heard the shout and flew to safety.

Answer the questions about the text.

1. How can you tell this is a folktale?

_____

_____

2. What literary element does the text include?

_____

3. What does the ant do for the dove? Why does he do this?

_____

_____

4. What do you think the lesson of this story is?

_____

_____

Name _____

A. Read the sentences from the passage. Then circle the antonym of the word in bold and write a simple definition for the word in bold on the line.

1. Jungles are **enormous**. It is easy to lose your way and feel tiny.

_____

2. He was **confused**. He heard the words again. In a moment, he understood that the bird was talking to him!

_____

3. The young boy **quickly** agreed to feed the bird. … His brother did not believe him at first. But finally he slowly agreed to go with the boy to meet the talking bird.

_____

B. Choose two words from the passage and use each word in a sentence. Use antonyms as context clues to define the words.

1. _____

_____

2. _____

_____

Name _____

A. Read each sentence and circle the word with the long *i* or long *u* sound. Write the word on the line.

1. The sun is very bright today. _____

2. I made a few clay animals in art class. _____

3. She tied a string around the box. _____

4. The gray kitten is so cute. _____

5. He can see that the sky will be gray. _____

B. Write the plural form of each noun on the line. Use the correct plural form from the word box. Mark the incorrectly spelled plural forms in the box with an *X*.

armies	ladies	ponies	relayes
relays	armys	ladys	cities
playes	cityes	plays	ponys

1. lady - y + ies = _____

2. relay + s = _____

3. army - y + ies = _____

4. pony - y + ies = _____

5. play + s = _____

6. city - y + ies = _____

Name _____

Evidence is details and examples from a text that support a writer's ideas. The student who wrote the paragraph below found text evidence that shows how the author uses what the characters do and say to share the theme of this folktale.

Topic sentence → In "Why People and Birds are Friends," the author uses what the characters do and say to share the theme about helping. At the beginning of the

Evidence → story, the brothers were lost and hungry. Then a bird says she will show them the way home if they feed her. The boys feed the bird, and the bird takes the

Concluding statement → brothers home. The author uses how the brothers and the bird help each other to share the message that when we help others, they often help us in return.

Write a paragraph about a folktale you have read. Find text evidence to show how the author uses what the characters do and say to share the theme, or message.

Write a topic sentence: _____

_____

Cite evidence from the text: _____

_____

_____

_____

End with a concluding statement: _____

_____

Name _____

A. Read the draft model. Use the questions that follow the draft to help you think about how you can use linking words to connect ideas.

Draft Model

I want to play a board game. My sister wants to play a video game. My mom wants us to clean up the yard.

1. What linking word would show how the first two ideas are different?

2. What linking word would connect the third idea to the first two ideas?

3. What other linking words could you add?

B. Now revise the draft by adding linking words to show how ideas are connected.

_____

_____

_____

_____

_____

Name _____

arrived	whispered	photographs	immigrated
inspected	moment	valuable	opportunity

Use a word from the box to answer each question. Then use the word in a sentence.

1. What is another word for *spoken in a very soft voice*? _____

    _____

2. What are the pictures taken by a camera? _____

    _____

3. What word might describe a chance for good things to happen?

    _____

4. What is another word for *a short amount of time*? _____

    _____

5. What word might describe something that is worth a lot of money?

    _____

6. What is another word for *looked at something closely*? _____

    _____

7. What word might describe that you got to where you were going?

    _____

8. What is another word for *came to a new country*? _____

    _____

Name _____

Read the selection. Complete the theme graphic organizer.

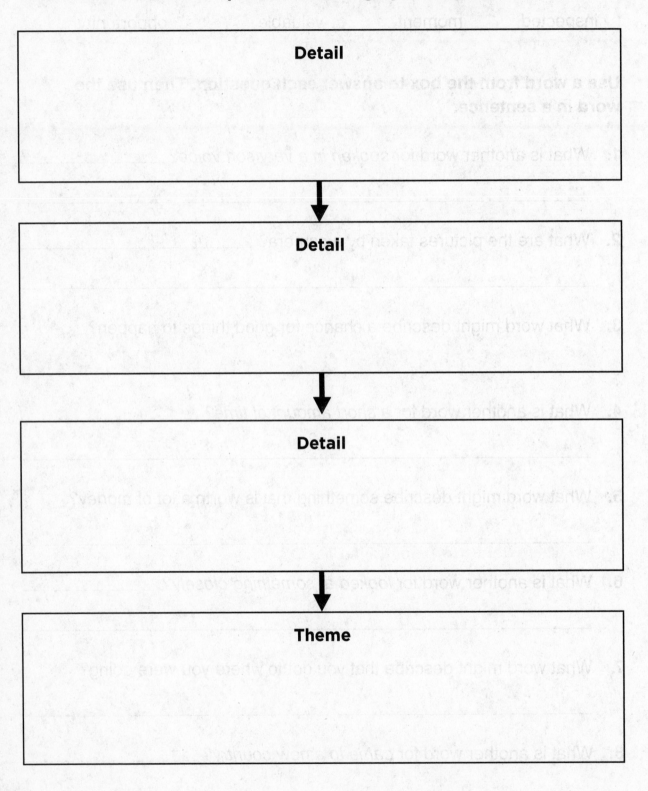

Detail

Detail

Detail

Theme

Name _____

Read the passage. Use the make, confirm, and revise predictions strategy to find clues to support predictions.

A Dream to the West

	Lan was eight years old in 1849. Life at home in China was tough,
14	and Yao, Lan's father, worked hard to put food on the table and make
28	a good life for his family.
34	Good news from the West gave hope. Word had spread that
45	people were getting rich finding gold in America, and Yao knew
56	that it was time to try for a better life. He made the trip by
71	himself at first. But after a few months, with a loan from family,
84	Lan and her mother were joining him.
91	Lan was as white as a ghost. "I'm scared, Mommy," she said.
103	"I only know my friends and family here in China, and I don't
116	even speak English."
119	"You'll settle in," her mom said. "Daddy will welcome us."
129	**The Golden Mountain**
132	"Daddy!" Lan came running to her father and gave him a big hug.
145	They took a long wagon trip in from the port in California to
158	where gold was being found.
163	"Are they really finding gold here?" Lan asked along the way.
174	"Some people have struck it rich!" Yao said. "They call the
185	area 'Gold Mountain.'"
188	The Gold Rush swept across America like wildfire when gold
198	was found in 1848. Now people from other countries immigrated.

"And what about our family in China?" she asked. "I'm going to miss them."

"I will send them money from my pay," he said. "Maybe one day they can join us here."

Many others did not have the money to send for their families. Lan knew she was lucky.

A New Life

Yao lived in a community with other Chinese people. When they arrived, Lan met Yao's friend, Chen, and Chen's daughter, Li. They walked around the village and talked.

"This is where we live and eat," Li said pointing. "And here is where we gather to talk."

Lan inspected the area. "Wow, I didn't know this many Chinese people lived here. They even speak Chinese!"

The discovery of gold gave hope to many immigrants.

"Yes, we have built a nice place to live," Yao said.

"But where is the mine that you work in, Daddy?" she asked.

"I don't work as a miner anymore, Lán," he said. "The hours were long, and we were not finding any gold. I now work as a shoemaker."

Lan knew life would not be the same, but she had hope. She looked around. The future was as open as the land.

"I'm just happy we're together," Lan said.

Name _____

A. Reread the passage and answer the questions.

1. What is one important detail about Lan's family in paragraph 2?

_____

_____

2. What is an important detail about Yao under the heading A New Life?

_____

_____

3. What is the theme of this passage?

_____

_____

B. Work with a partner. Read the passage aloud. Pay attention to rate. Stop after one minute. Fill out the chart.

	Words Read	−	Number of Errors	=	Words Correct Score
First Read		−		=	
Second Read		−		=	

Name _____

A Long Wait on Angel Island

It was November 24, 1924. My mother and I arrived in America from China twelve days ago. We stayed in a room with many women. Then a guard took me to a small room where a man sat at a table. The man began to speak in a language I didn't understand. Then he spoke in my own language. He asked me my name and with whom we will stay in America.

Answer the questions about the text.

1. **How can you tell that this is historical fiction?**

   _____

2. **When does this story take place? How does the illustration help you know this?**

   _____

   _____

3. **How does the illustration help you better understand the main character?**

   _____

   _____

Name _____

Read each sentence below. Underline the things that are compared in each simile. Then write what the simile means on the line.

1. Lan was as white as a ghost.

   _____

2. The Gold Rush swept across America like wildfire when gold was found in 1848.

   _____

3. The future was as open as the land.

   _____

4. The gold shined like the sun.

   _____

5. Down in the mine it was as black as night.

   _____

Name _____

A. Read each set of words and listen for the long e sound. Circle all the words with the long e sound in each row.

1. street   freeze   pest   mend

2. spend   creek   when   weak

3. field   heel   shelf   cream

4. lend   green   fresh   speaks

5. bean   bent   seal   team

B. Circle the word with the inflectional ending that is spelled correctly. Write the word on the line.

1. He _____ his name and address on the line.

   copyd   copyed   copied

2. The wet laundry _____ on the clothesline.

   dries   drys   dryies

3. We are _____ than we have ever been.

   happyer   happier   happyier

4. That is the _____ sink I have ever seen!

   leakyest   leakyiest   leakiest

5. Have you _____ to the party invitation yet?

   replyed   replied   replyd

Name _____

Evidence is details and examples from a text that support a writer's opinion. This student wrote an opinion about whether or not the author gives enough information to help him understand the story's theme.

Topic sentence →   In "A Dream to the West," the author uses what Lan and her family do and say to share the theme that dreams can come true if you work hard. At

Evidence → the beginning of the story, Lan and her family were dreaming of a better life. Lan's father went to America. He worked very hard and saved money so Lan and her mother could go. When Lan gets to her new home, she sees that her family has a better

Concluding statement → life now. The author uses what Lan and her family say and do to help me understand the story's theme about working hard to make dreams come true.

Write your opinion about a story you read. Find text evidence to support your opinion of how the author uses what the characters do and say to share the theme, or message.

Write a topic sentence: _____

_____

Cite evidence from the text: _____

_____

_____

_____

End with a concluding statement: _____

_____

Name _____

A. Read the draft model. Use the questions that follow the draft to help you think about what precise nouns you can add.

Draft Model

Once, a family moved to a new town. They traveled a long time in their car to get to the town. When they got to their new house, they unpacked their things. Then they met their neighbors.

---

1. What precise nouns could be used to help make the story clearer for the reader?

2. What nouns would help readers visualize the characters, the town, and the house?

3. What nouns could be used to describe the journey?

4. What sorts of things does the family unpack?

B. Now revise the draft by adding precise nouns to help make the story about the family easier for readers to understand.

_____

_____

_____

_____

_____

_____

Name _____

independent	elect	decisions	announced
candidates	government	estimate	convince

Finish each sentence using the vocabulary word provided.

1. **(estimate)** Just by quickly looking in the room, _____

_____ .

2. **(convince)** When I wanted a pet _____

_____ .

3. **(announced)** On the loud speakers _____

_____ .

4. **(government)** To help guide our nation, _____

_____ .

5. **(candidates)** When she ran for mayor, _____

_____ .

6. **(independent)** Even though the girl was shy, _____

_____ .

7. **(decisions)** When I decided to take the extra classes, _____

_____ .

8. **(elect)** If you want to be a politician, _____

_____ .

Name _____

Read the selection. Complete the author's point of view graphic organizer.

Details

↓

Point of View

Name _____

Read the passage. Use the reread strategy to make sure you understand the text.

Express Yourself

Do you tell friends who you think the best singer is? Do you
13 wear a T-shirt for a team you like? This may not seem unusual.
26 It is your right to say what you think. Yet, there have been
39 people who have had to prove their freedom of speech.

49 **Speak Your Mind**

52 Freedom of speech is the right to tell what you think. This is a
66 right in the Constitution. Even if other people do not agree, you
78 should still have the right to say what you think.

88 To speak your thoughts does not just mean saying them. It can
100 mean what you do. There were students in 1969 who "spoke"
111 with actions. America was at war then. The students did not like
123 the war. They wanted to show how they felt. So they wore black
136 armbands.

137 Some people did not like the bands. The students went to
148 court. This case was called *Tinker v. Des Moines*. The court said
160 that the students could wear the bands to school. It was their
172 freedom of speech. The students could wear the bands even if
183 others disagreed.

Name _____

Are There Limits?

There are times when free speech is not allowed. If telling your beliefs is unsafe to others, it is unprotected by the Constitution. What if you shout "fire"? If there is not a fire, this is not free speech. You are causing trouble. People might get hurt.

The government will not allow this. A person who does this will be punished. This happened in 1919. The case was called *Schenck v. United States*.

When our country was new and people were given freedom of speech, it was good. They were independent. They could speak their minds. There have been times when free speech has hurt people. The government can help define free speech by how people use it.

Free speech is your right. Yet, if people get hurt, it is not allowed. This means that people make the government work by using their free speech. They speak their beliefs. They do this within the rules of the law. Sometimes, the government has to redefine how people use this freedom.

Because of free speech you can make your beliefs known. People will continue to help define the rules of government by reviewing their rights.

Name _____

A. Reread the passage and answer the questions.

1. **What does the second paragraph tell you about how the author feels about free speech?**

   _____

   _____

2. **How do you think the author would have felt about the students in the third and fourth paragraphs being able to wear black armbands?**

   _____

   _____

3. **How does your point of view about free speech compare with the author's?**

   _____

   _____

   _____

B. Work with a partner. Read the passage aloud. Pay attention to accuracy and phrasing. Stop after one minute. Fill out the chart.

	Words Read	–	Number of Errors	=	Words Correct Score
First Read		–		=	
Second Read		–		=	

Name _____

Women in Congress

Today, many members of the United States Congress are women. It hasn't always been that way. No women had ever served in Congress before 1916. That year, Jeanette Rankin from Montana was the first woman to be elected to the House of Representatives. She was elected even before women had the right to vote. Then in 1922, Rebecca Felton from Georgia became the first female senator.

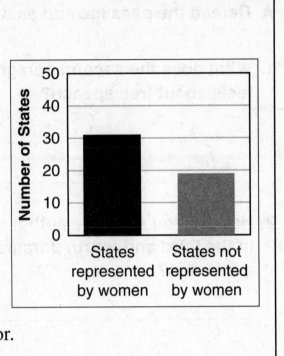

Answer the questions about the text.

1. How can you tell this is expository text?

_____

_____

2. What two text features does the text include?

_____

_____

3. What is the text's heading? What heading might the text feature have?

_____

_____

4. What does the bar graph tell you?

_____

_____

Name _____

Study the information about prefixes in the box below. Then underline the word in each sentence that contains one of the prefixes listed. Next, define the word on the line provided.

> *re-* means "to do again"
>
> *dis-* means "not" or "opposite"
>
> *un-* means "not" or "opposite"

1. My dog does not like the snow, so it was unusual to see him playing in it

this winter. _____

2. The two brothers disagreed. One brother said cheetahs are the fastest

animal, and one brother said lions are. _____

3. We are reviewing Chapter 1 for the test next Monday. _____

_____

4. The jungle is full of wild animals, so it is unsafe to walk there alone.

_____

5. If you don't wear knee pads when you skate, your knees are unprotected.

_____

6. Even though I knew the meaning of the word, I had to redefine it for the

class. _____

Name _____

A. Read each sentence. Circle the word that begins with a silent letter. Write the word on the line and place an X over the silent letter.

1. I know how to ice-skate. _____

2. I wrote my name on the paper. _____

3. I saw the mouse gnaw on the cheese. _____

4. I will knit a scarf for my mom. _____

5. A wren made a nest in the tree. _____

B. Read each sentence. Circle the word that is the correct singular or plural possessive noun.

1. The (dog's, dogs') bowl needs more water.

2. The (mens', men's) softball game is today.

3. This is my (friends's, friend's) bike.

4. All the (people's, peoples') work was amazing.

5. My (mom's, moms') car is in the garage.

Name _____

Evidence is details and examples from a text that support a writer's ideas. This student wrote about how the author uses details to support his point of view that free speech is important.

Topic sentence → In "Express Yourself," the author uses details to support his point of view that free speech is important. The author says that Americans have the

Evidence → right to say what they think. He believes that free speech is a good thing as long as people follow the rules of the law. For example, the author says that naming your favorite singer is a good example of free speech. The author also says that yelling "fire" when there is not a fire is dangerous. The author

Concluding statement → uses details to support his point of view that free speech is an important right of all Americans, as long as they follow the rules. I agree with the author. It is important to be able to share how you feel.

Write a paragraph about a text you read. Find text evidence to support the author's point of view. Then write about your point of view.

Write a topic sentence: _____

_____

Cite evidence from the text: _____

_____

_____

End with a concluding statement: _____

_____

Name _____

A. Read the draft model. Use the questions that follow the draft to help you think about what supporting details you can add.

Draft Model

Many schools have elections. Kids vote for their favorite candidate. These elections are usually held sometime in the fall. Voting is important.

---

1. What kinds of elections do schools hold?

2. What offices are candidates running for? What supporting details would describe the campaigns?

3. Why are elections held in the fall?

4. What detail would tell why voting is important?

B. Now revise the draft by adding facts, definitions, and other details to help readers learn more about school elections.

_____

_____

_____

_____

_____

_____

Name _____

population	recognized	success	resources
caretakers	relatives	survive	threatened

Use a word from the box to answer each question. Then use the word in a sentence.

1. What word might describe a great performance? _____

    _____

2. What word describes all the people living in the same place?

    _____

3. What is another word for *in danger of being hurt*? _____

    _____

4. Who are the people at a zoo that keep the animals safe? _____

    _____

5. What are your cousins, aunts, and uncles? _____

    _____

6. What is another word for *remembered a person from the past*?

    _____

7. What word might describe staying alive after a dangerous event?

    _____

8. What are the things that are available to be used when needed?

    _____

Name _____

Read the selection. Complete the author's point of view graphic organizer.

Details

↓

Point of View

Name _____

Read the passage. Use the reread strategy to make sure you understand the text.

The Sound of Elephants

A Love of Sounds

4	Katy Payne loves to listen to all kinds of sounds. She loves to
17	listen to music, of course. But mostly, she listens to animals. And
29	she has spent most of her life doing it. By listening to them she
43	has helped them live on.
48	Katy first studied whales and the wonderful sounds they make
58	under the water. Some people call them "whale songs." They
68	sound like strange music. Katy knew that elephants were like
78	whales in some ways. They were both large creatures. And they
89	both cared for their young. Katy wanted to study elephants, too.

Hidden Sounds
100	
102	Katy went to a zoo to see and hear the elephants. She watched
115	and listened. She liked to hear the sounds they made. There were
127	loud sounds and soft sounds. They hummed and made trumpet
137	sounds. The sounds made Katy think of whale songs. She knew
148	that whales sometimes made sounds that she could not hear. That
159	gave Katy a great idea. What if elephants make hidden sounds
170	too? She went to find out.

Name _____

First, Katy taped the sounds of elephants. Then she took the tapes to a lab. She used a computer to make pictures of the sound waves. The pictures showed sounds that Katy could not hear. The elephants were making hidden sounds! No one had ever seen hidden sounds from elephants. Katy had found something special.

Helping by Hearing

Katy became worried about elephants. People and elephants do not always live well near each other. Sometimes elephants eat people's crops, and people get angry.

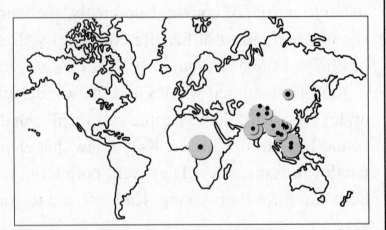

Elephants live in the wild in Africa and Asia.

Sometimes careless people build homes on land that elephants use. It is hard for these elephants to survive. Katy wanted the two to be able to live near each other.

Katy started a project with some friends. They listen to the sounds of elephants to get to know them better. This helps people know more. They are hopeful that the more people understand elephants, the more they will want to help.

Katy also uses the sounds to count the elephants. She has found that there are fewer now than there used to be. Some people have heard about this. They have started helpful projects of their own. Now more people are helping elephants. And it's all because of good people like Katy Payne!

Name _____

A. Reread the passage and answer the questions.

1. How does the author feel about Katy Payne's idea in paragraph three?

_____

_____

2. How does the author feel about Katy's discovery that elephants were making hidden sounds?

_____

_____

_____

3. What is the author's point of view about Katy?

_____

_____

_____

B. Work with a partner. Read the passage aloud. Pay attention to rate. Stop after one minute. Fill out the chart.

	Words Read	–	Number of Errors	=	Words Correct Score
First Read		–		=	
Second Read		–		=	

Name _____

PAWS: People Helping Animals

PAWS is a group of people that helps animals. They care for homeless pets and find new homes for them. They care for hurt wild animals and return the animals to the wild when they are healthy. PAWS also teaches people how to care for pets and wild animals. They work to pass laws that are good for animals.

You Can Help, Too!

Read books that tell you how to care for pets and other animals.

Lawrence M. Sawyer/Getty Images

A PAWS worker cares for a homeless animal at a shelter.

Answer the questions about the text.

1. How can you tell this is expository text?

   _____

2. What two text features does the text include?

   _____

3. What is the text's heading? What does it tell you about the text?

   _____

4. What does the sidebar tell you about PAWS? What other information does it give?

   _____

   _____

Name _____

Read each sentence below. Underline the suffix of the word in bold and write the word's definition on the line. Then write your own sentence using the word in bold.

1. Katy first studied whales and the **wonderful** sounds they make under the water.

_____

_____

_____

2. Sometimes **careless** people build homes on land that elephants use.

_____

_____

_____

3. They are **hopeful** that the more people understand elephants, the more they will want to help.

_____

_____

_____

4. They have started **helpful** projects of their own.

_____

_____

_____

Name _____

A. Circle the word with a three-letter blend to complete each sentence.

1. Please use a _____ to drink your orange juice.

   cup   straw   glass

2. Dad _____ the car with soap and water to clean it.

   washes   soaks   scrubs

3. We should go outside and _____ the ball around.

   throw   toss   kick

4. Our hamster likes to _____ when he is hungry.

   chatter   squeak   click

5. I will _____ this orange in half if you want to share it.

   divide   slice   split

B. Write the word that has two closed syllables. Draw a slanted line (/) between the syllables.

1. basket   bonus   _____

2. sudden   acorn   _____

3. baby   mitten   _____

4. napkin   pilot   _____

5. major   magnet   _____

Name _____

Evidence is details and examples from a text that support a writer's opinion. This student wrote about whether or not the author uses details to support her point of view that Katy Payne is the reason more people are helping elephants.

Topic sentence → In "The Sound of Elephants," the author uses details to support her point of view that Katy Payne's work is helping elephants survive. Katy
Evidence → studied elephants and discovered that they make hidden sounds. The author says that Katy found something special. Katy started a project that helped people understand elephants better. The author thinks that because of Katy's discovery more people are interested in helping elephants. The author uses
Concluding statement → details to support her point of view. I agree. Katy's discovery turned into a way to get more people involved with helping elephants.

Write about a text you read. Find text evidence to support your opinion about the author's point of view. Then write about how your point of view compares with the author's.

Write a topic sentence: _____

_____

Cite evidence from the text: _____

_____

_____

End with a concluding statement: _____

_____

Name _____

A. Read the draft model. Use the questions that follow the draft to help you think about what sequence words you can add to help make the order of events clear.

Draft Model

There was a duck with an injured wing in our yard. We called a man at the animal shelter. He came and wrapped its wing. The wing healed. He took the duck back to its home in the lake.

---

1. When did the narrator call the animal shelter?

2. What sequence words can be added to help organize the other events of the story?

3. What sequence words can be used to give the writing a clear beginning, middle, and end?

B. Now revise the draft by adding sequence words to help make the story of the duck easy to follow.

_____

_____

_____

_____

_____

_____

Name _____

| inventor | observer | bounce | imagine |

Use the context clues in each sentence to help you decide which vocabulary word fits best in the blank.

Lawrence was fascinated as he watched the crew at the construction site in town. A new office building was being built, and Lawrence had been an _____ all summer.

"Today's the day it is finally done," he told his friend Walter, standing next to him.

"Wow!" said Walter. "It's been so long."

They gazed up at the tall glass building. "Yes, when I first saw them knocking the old building down with a wrecking ball, I thought the ball would _____ right off the brick!" Lawrence said. "But that was just the beginning of the fun."

Lawrence loved to _____ himself wearing a hard hat, hammering, and putting up walls. He admired the skill of the workers and the tools they used. "The _____ of all of those tools must have been very smart," he said. "They are all so useful."

"And look at the results," Walter said. "The building is beautiful."

"Yes it is," Lawrence said as he smiled. "Maybe one day, I'll be out there helping."

Name _____

Read the selection. Complete the point of view graphic organizer.

Details

Point of View

Name _____

Read the poem. Check your understanding by asking yourself how the narrator thinks or feels.

Learning to Read

	When I began reading,
4	a book was like a bowl
10	of letter soup.
13	As and Bs mixed with Ps and Qs.
21	The letters stirred together
25	like a thick, messy mush.
30	Not one word spoke to me
36	in any language I understood.
41	So I brought books to my mom and dad
50	like gifts for a long time. They cut out hours
60	for me from their days and nights. They knew
69	I needed to know what every word meant
77	so the words could be part of my life. Not right
88	away, but sooner than I thought,
94	letters let themselves be led into lines
101	that looked like the words I heard in my head.
111	Now the world seems smaller, somehow.
117	I figured out how to read and the words bring
127	the whole world of incredible things
133	into my open hands, curious as cats.

Name _____

A. Reread the passage and answer the questions.

1. Who is the narrator of this poem?

_____

_____

_____

2. What is the narrator's point of view?

_____

_____

_____

3. How do you know what the narrator's point of view is?

_____

_____

_____

B. Work with a partner. Read the passage aloud. Pay attention to phrasing. Stop after one minute. Fill out the chart.

	Words Read	–	Number of Errors	=	Words Correct Score
First Read		–		=	
Second Read		–		=	

Name _____

Missing Glasses

I looked in the pile of clothes.
I checked the case where it usually goes.
I searched all around
but I finally found
that my glasses were right on my nose.

Answer the questions about the poem.

1. What literary element of this poem makes it a limerick?

_____

2. Which lines rhyme?

_____

_____

3. What is the poem about?

_____

4. Where does the speaker find her glasses?

_____

_____

Name _____

Read the lines of free verse below. Then answer the questions.

Learning to Read
So I brought books to my mom and dad
like gifts for a long time. They cut out hours
for me from their days and nights. They knew
I needed to know what every word meant

so the words could be part of my life. Not right
away, but sooner than I thought,
letters let themselves be led into lines
that looked like the words I heard in my head.

Now the world seems smaller, somehow.
I figured out how to read and the words bring
the whole world of incredible things
into my open hands, curious as cats.

1. **Find an example of rhyme in the poem.**

   _____

2. **Write an example of alliteration from the poem on the lines below.**

   _____

   _____

3. **Write another line for this poem that includes alliteration or rhyme.**

   _____

   _____

   _____

Name _____

**Read each passage. Write the simile on the line. Then write the
two things that are being compared.**

1. The letters stirred together
   like a thick, messy mush.

   _____

   _____

   _____

2. When I began reading,
   a book was like a bowl
   of letter soup.

   _____

   _____

   _____

3. So I brought books to my mom and dad
   like gifts for a long time.

   _____

   _____

   _____

Name _____

A. Circle the word with a digraph to complete each sentence. Underline the digraph in that word. Write the word on the line.

1. I got a new _____ for my birthday.

    coat   watch   bike

2. We fed the baby _____ at the farm.

    chicks   ponies   cows

3. This year for the talent show, I plan to _____.

    juggle   dance   sing

4. My grandpa has a huge _____ collection.

    coin   shell   art

5. I got purple paint on my _____.

    thumb   elbow   face

B. An open syllable has a CV pattern and usually has a long vowel sound. Circle the word that has one or more open syllables. Then write the syllables on the lines.

1. private   rabbit   _____   _____

2. napkin   fable   _____   _____

3. moment   minute   _____   _____

4. follow   tiger   _____   _____

Name _____

Evidence is details and examples from a text that support a writer's ideas. This student wrote about how the author's choice of words helps us understand what the narrator thinks about learning to read.

Topic sentence ⟶   In "Learning the Read," the author chooses words that help us understand what the narrator thinks about learning to read. The narrator uses the words

Evidence ⟶ "letter soup" to describe reading. When I think about letter soup, I think about letters floating all over the place in no order. Then the narrator learns to read and says that the "letters let themselves be led into lines." That means the letters are now words. I read that reading brings the whole world into the narrator's open hands. The author chooses

Concluding statement ⟶ words that help me understand what the narrator thinks about learning to read.

Write about a poem you read. Find text evidence to support the author's word choice when telling about the narrator's point of view.

Write a topic sentence: _____

_____

Cite evidence from the text: _____

_____

_____

End with a concluding statement: _____

_____

Name _____

A. Read the draft model. Use the questions that follow the draft to help you think about descriptive details you can add.

Draft Model

Our lawn mower is a good machine. It is loud and gives a deep growl when you turn it on. When the grass is shaggy, I use the lawn mower to give the grass a haircut. It is a very helpful machine to have around.

1. In the first sentence what is a better word than "good" to describe a lawn mower?

2. Does the growl of the lawn mower sound like the growls of something else?

3. What does the machine look like?

4. Can you describe how the lawn mower looks or feels when it is cutting the grass?

B. Now revise the draft by adding details to describe the lawn mower.

_____

_____

_____

_____

_____

_____

Name _____

| disbelief | dismay | fabulous | features |
| offered | splendid | unique | watchful |

Use the context clues in each sentence to help you decide which vocabulary word fits best. Write the word in the blank.

Mom was in _____ when she saw the state of the

living room, unable to understand what had happened. She looked

around with _____ at the broken lamp, the stains on the

_____, one-of-a-kind carpet, and the footprints on the sofa.

My brother and I _____ her some stories about what had

happened. We described the _____ of the animal that had

done the damage. "Um, it had a _____, beautiful coat like a

Golden Retriever and a _____, curled tail like a snake! It was

the most incredible thing we had ever seen!"

Finally, under Mom's _____ eye, we cleaned up. There was

no creature, just us, playing outdoor games in the living room.

Name _____

Read the selection. Complete the problem and solution graphic organizer.

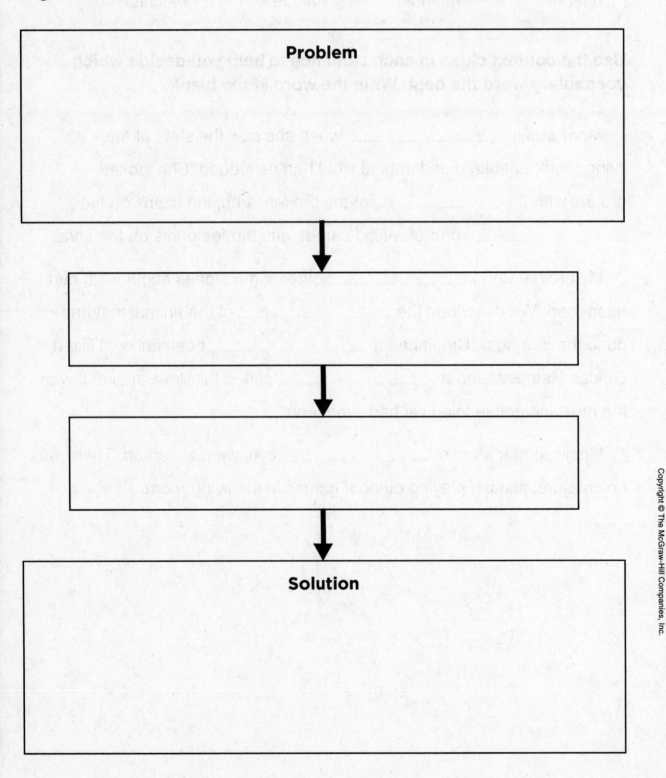

Problem

Solution

Name _____

Read the passage. Use the visualize strategy to help you understand what you are reading.

How Zebras Got Their Stripes

This story happened a long time ago in Africa. One day,
11 Baboon, who was very fierce, decided to leave the jungle tree
22 where he lived. He wanted to live next to the river. He was so
36 mean that he told all the other animals that the land belonged to
49 him. Baboon stated he was the only one allowed to drink from
61 the river.

63 The animals were upset. They were sad because they needed
73 water to survive. But all of them were afraid of Baboon. He had a
87 big head with thick eyebrows and long teeth. He showed his teeth
99 every chance he got to scare the other animals. They didn't know
111 what to do.

114 Zebra was young and brave. He was fearless and handsome in
125 his pure white coat. In the old days, zebras had all white coats.
138 Zebra said to the other animals, "I am not afraid of Baboon. I
151 will tell him we are going to drink from the river." The next day,
165 Zebra met with Baboon, but Baboon refused to talk to Zebra.
176 So Zebra challenged Baboon to a fight. Baboon laughed. It had
187 been a long time since he had lost a fight.

197 They agreed that the loser of the fight would have to leave the
210 jungle and river. He would have to live on the barren hill. The
223 empty hill was not a place anyone wanted to live. They would
235 meet the next morning in Baboon's yard next to the river.

Name _____

The next day, Zebra came to Baboon's yard. Baboon had built a bonfire. Zebra's white coat glowed in the sun. It looked like Zebra was lit from inside his body. All the animals came to watch the fight. They knew that it would be difficult to beat Baboon.

Baboon and Zebra were both strong and used all of their skills. They knew what they were good at. Zebra used his powerful legs to run at Baboon. But Baboon was very swift. He used his quickness to jump out of Zebra's way. Before Zebra could stop, he was suddenly close to the bonfire. He was so close that the heat from the fire began to burn him.

Zebra turned around and kicked Baboon over the river and onto the empty hill. He wasn't injured, but his pride was hurt. He knew he had lost. The animals could drink from the river.

Zebra won, but he was left with marks. The fire had burned long black stripes on his white coat. From that day on, all zebras had black stripes and were proud of them. They were a symbol that Zebra had fought and won to keep water free for all animals.

Name _____

A. Reread the passage and answer the questions.

1. What is the problem in this story?

_____

_____

_____

2. What solution does Zebra come up with?

_____

_____

_____

3. What are the results of this solution?

_____

_____

_____

B. Work with a partner. Read the passage aloud. Pay attention to expression. Stop after one minute. Fill out the chart.

	Words Read	–	Number of Errors	=	Words Correct Score
First Read		–		=	
Second Read		–		=	

Name _____

How Bear Lost His Tail

Long ago, Bear had a long, shiny tail. He was proud of his tail and bragged, "No other tail in the forest can compare with mine!"

Fox got tired of Bear's bragging. One winter day, Fox went to a frozen lake and sat by a hole in the ice. When he heard Bear coming, Fox said loudly to himself, "My tail just isn't shiny enough to catch that juicy fish under the ice." Then he hid behind a tree.

"My shiny tail could catch that fish!" Bear thought, licking his lips. He dipped his tail into the icy water. While waiting, Bear fell asleep.

Fox watched Bear sleep. Then Fox crept up behind him and shouted as loud as he could, "Wake up, Bear! The fish is biting your tail!" Bear woke with such a start that his frozen tail snapped clean off.

Answer the questions about the text.

1. How do you know this text is a folktale?

_____

2. What problem does Fox face?

_____

3. How does Fox solve his problem?

_____

4. What do you think the lesson of this text is?

_____

Name _____

Read the sentences from the passage. Circle the synonyms in the sentences that help you define each word in bold. Then in your own words, write the definition of the word on the line.

1. The animals were **upset**. They were sad because they needed water to survive.

   _____

2. Zebra was young and **brave**. He was fearless and handsome in his pure white coat.

   _____

3. He would have to live on the **barren** hill. The empty hill was not a place anyone wanted to live.

   _____

4. But Baboon was very **swift**. He used his quickness to jump out of Zebra's way.

   _____

5. He wasn't **injured**, but his pride was hurt. He knew he had lost. The animals could drink from the river.

   _____

Name _____

A. Read each sentence and underline the word with an *r*-controlled vowel sound. Write the word on the line and circle the vowel + *r* combination that makes the sound.

1. Today is the third day of my vacation. _____

2. At camp we will learn to row a canoe. _____

3. Will you help me serve lunch today? _____

4. It hurt to find out that the team lost again. _____

5. I plan to move the fern to a sunny window. _____

B. Read each pair of words below. Then write the contraction from the box that matches each pair.

didn't	can't	I'm	he's	isn't	we'll

1. is not _____

2. we will _____

3. can not _____

4. I am _____

5. did not _____

6. he is _____

Name _____

> *Evidence* is details and examples from a text that support a writer's ideas. The student who wrote the paragraph below found text evidence that shows how the author uses steps Zebra takes to solve a problem and to explain how something happened.
>
> **Topic sentence** →   In "How Zebras Got Their Stripes," the author uses how Zebra solves a problem to explain why zebras have stripes. At the beginning of the story, the animals were upset because Baboon said they couldn't drink from the river. This is a problem because animals need water to live. I read that Zebra and Baboon agreed to fight. Zebra fell into Baboon's fire. When he jumped out, he was covered with marks. Zebra won and the problem was solved. But now, all zebras have stripes. The author explains why zebras have stripes by using what Zebra says and does to solve a problem.
>
> **Evidence** →
>
> **Concluding statement** →

Write about a folktale you have read. Find text evidence to show how the author uses how the character solves a problem to explain something.

Write a topic sentence: _____

_____

Cite evidence from the text: _____

_____

_____

_____

End with a concluding statement: _____

_____

Name _____

A. Read the draft model. Use the questions that follow the draft to help you think about what sentence types you can add to make the story more interesting.

Draft Model

I like butterflies. My favorites are monarch butterflies. They lay their eggs on milkweed plants. I think everyone should plant some milkweed in their yard today. I wonder who else likes butterflies too.

---

1. How could you rewrite the first sentence to make it exclamatory?

2. How could you rewrite the fourth sentence to make it imperative?

3. How could you rewrite the last sentence to make it interrogative?

B. Now revise the draft by using different types of sentences to make the story about monarch butterflies more interesting to read and easier to understand.

_____

_____

_____

_____

_____

_____

Name _____

amazement	disappear	leader	refused
bravery	donated	nervous	temporary

Use a word from the box to answer each question. Then use the word in a sentence.

1. What word can describe the ability to face danger without fear?

   _____

2. What is another word for *worried*? _____

   _____

3. What word means *to become impossible to see any longer*? _____

   _____

4. What did the girl do when she turned down the money she was offered?

   _____

5. What word describes someone who shows the way? _____

   _____

6. What did the children do when they gave their money to a charity?

   _____

7. What is another word for *wonder*? _____

   _____

8. What word describes something that lasts for a short time? _____

   _____

Name _____

Read the selection. Complete the cause and effect graphic organizer.

Characters

Setting

Cause	Effect

Cause	Effect

Cause	Effect

Name _____

Read the passage. Use the visualize strategy to help you understand the text.

A Letter to Helen Keller

Dear Ms. Keller,

3	My name is Amelia Grant. I live in Nome, TX, where my
15	daddy runs an oil factory. I was born in the year 1900, so I am
30	now twelve years old. When I was eight, I was out near one of the
45	oil wells. There was a huge explosion. I was real close to it. As a
60	result, I lost most of my hearing.
67	A lot has changed for me since then. For one, I cannot hear
80	music in the same way. I used to love listening to my mother sing
94	songs. When I first lost my hearing, I was sad that I would never
108	again hear my mother sing. But now I put my ear to her chest. I
123	can feel the vibrations of her voice. Now, I feel music instead of
136	hearing it.
138	Also, I have to go to a different school a long stretch away
151	from our hometown. It is called Texas School for the Deaf. It is
164	in the city of Austin, two hundred miles away from Nome. The
176	teachers are kind, but I spend months at a time away from my
189	family. I get to see them during holidays, but I sure do miss them.
203	During our last winter holiday, my daddy gave me a book you
215	wrote, *The Story of My Life*. I read that when you first became
228	deaf and blind, you had a hard time showing people what you
240	wanted. Because of this, you would sometimes get mad and make
251	loud noises.

Name _____

Your mom and dad were frustrated. You really drove your parents up the wall! So that's why they found a great teacher for you. Her name was Ms. Sullivan. She showed you that there was a word to describe every object and idea. Because of Ms. Sullivan, you are now able to read and write by touch.

I also read that you love to ask questions. So now, when we are learning in school, I ask lots of questions. I found out that this really helps me learn. I am learning more now than I ever did before I lost my hearing. Maybe mother is right when she says "every cloud has a silver lining." Even when something seems really bad, a good thing can come from it.

I have a best friend in Nome. Her name is Anna Bailey. When I lost my hearing, I thought Anna might not be my friend anymore. I thought she might want to play only with people who could hear. But I was wrong. Anna stayed friends with me. She even helped me. She told me I would get used to being deaf. "It might take some time," she said. "But you'll find your feet." She made me feel much better.

When I first heard about you, I was amazed. Even though you are deaf and blind, you can do almost anything! You even went to college. You are like a hero to me. I hope that one day I can visit you and we can learn more about each other.

Sincerely,
Amelia Grant

A. Reread the passage and answer the questions.

1. Describe two things that changed for Amelia after she lost her hearing.

_____

_____

_____

2. Reread the fifth paragraph of the letter. How did Helen Keller learn to read by touch?

_____

_____

_____

3. What made Amelia start asking lots of questions in school?

_____

_____

B. Work with a partner. Read the passage aloud. Pay attention to phrasing. Stop after one minute. Fill out the chart.

	Words Read	–	Number of Errors	=	Words Correct Score
First Read		–		=	
Second Read		–		=	

Name _____

A Surprise Visit

One hot Saturday in the summer of 1945, my friend Henry and I were playing baseball in the park. Suddenly Henry shouted, "Look! That's the Kansas City Monarchs' bus across the street!" The team members got off, and two came walking toward us. One of them was the new shortstop, Jackie Robinson. He called out, "Keep batting. I'll check your swing."

Answer the questions about the text.

1. How do you know this text is historical fiction?

_____

_____

2. What text feature does the text include?

_____

_____

3. How does the text feature help show that the text is historical fiction?

_____

_____

4. How else can you tell the text takes place in the past?

_____

_____

Name _____

Read each passage below. Circle the context clues that help you understand each idiom in bold. Then write the meaning of the idiom on the line.

1. Also, I have to go to a different school **a long stretch** away from our hometown. It is called Texas School for the Deaf. It is in the city of Austin, two hundred miles away from Nome.

   _____

2. Your mom and dad were frustrated. You really **drove your parents up the wall**! So that's why they found a great teacher for you.

   _____

3. I am learning more now than I ever did before I lost my hearing. Maybe mother is right when she says "**every cloud has a silver lining**." Even when something seems really bad, a good thing can come from it.

   _____

4. Anna stayed friends with me. She even helped me. She told me I would get used to being deaf. "It might take some time," she said. "But you'll **find your feet**."

   _____

Name _____

A. Read each sentence. Underline the word that has the /är/ or /ôr/ vowel sound. Then circle the letters in the word that make the sound.

1. We counted five trees in the yard.

2. After walking three miles my legs became sore.

3. Ice hockey is his favorite sport.

4. I can see a shark in the distance.

5. It is better to share than it is to hoard.

6. The man uses only wood to carve the boxes.

B. The prefix *pre-* means *before*. The prefix *re-* means *again*. The prefix *un-* means *not*. Read each question. Circle the correct answer.

1. Which word means "heat before"?

preheat   heater   reheat

2. Which word means "not kind"?

kindly   unkind   kindness

3. Which word means "read again"?

reread   preread   reader

4. Which word means "not usual"?

unusual   usually   reuse

5. Which word means "pay before"?

repay   payment   prepay

Name _____

Evidence is details and examples from a text that support a writer's opinion. This student wrote an opinion about how well the author uses signal words to show causes and effects in time order.

Topic sentence →   In "A Letter to Helen Keller," the author does a good job using signal words to show causes and effects in time order. At the beginning of the letter,

Evidence → Amelia writes about a huge explosion. As a result, she lost most of her hearing. The signal words help me understand that the explosion caused Amelia to lose her hearing. Amelia read about how Helen Keller asked lots of questions in school. So she asks

Concluding statement → lots of questions, too. The author's use of signal words helped me find causes and effects in Amelia's letter and understand the events of her life in time order.

Write your opinion about a story you read. Find text evidence to support your opinion of how the author uses signal words to show cause and effect in the story.

Write a topic sentence: _____

_____

Cite evidence from the text: _____

_____

_____

_____

End with a concluding statement: _____

_____

Name _____

A. Read the draft model. Use the questions that follow the draft to help you think about what linking words and phrases you can add to help connect ideas.

Draft Model

I did not want to play piano anymore. It was too hard. My piano teacher explained to me the importance of music. He inspired me. Now I really enjoy playing piano.

---

1. What linking words and phrases could you add to make relationships clearer to the reader?

2. What linking words and phrases would show when events happened?

3. What linking words and phrases would make the text easier to follow?

B. Now revise the draft by adding linking words to help connect ideas.

_____

_____

_____

_____

_____

_____

Name _____

warmth	globe	surface	solar system
support	temperature	amount	astronomy

Finish each sentence using the vocabulary word provided.

1. **(support)** I depend on _____

   _____ .

2. **(amount)** The sign above the oranges _____

   _____ .

3. **(solar system)** The Sun and the planets _____

   _____ .

4. **(surface)** Digging deep below _____

   _____ .

5. **(temperature)** In order for the water to boil, _____

   _____ .

6. **(globe)** If you want to see _____

   _____ .

7. **(astronomy)** If you like to look at the night sky, _____

   _____ .

8. **(warmth)** Most plants need _____

   _____ .

Name _____

Read the selection. Complete the main idea and key details graphic organizer.

Main Idea
Detail
Detail
Detail

Name _____

Read the passage. Use the summarize strategy to check your understanding of important details of the passage.

Seeing Red

12	You have probably seen stars in the sky. Maybe you even saw
23	a planet. Have you wondered what other planets are like? Others
34	have, too. In the search to answer this question, scientists have
45	learned a lot about Mars. Scientists will do everything they can
	to learn even more about Mars.
51	**Fourth Place**
53	Mars is the fourth planet from the sun. Earth is the third
65	planet. Mars has a reddish color. It is called the Red Planet. It is
79	about half the size of Earth. Earth has different types of climates.
91	There are cold, hot, dry, and wet places. Mars is just a cold
104	desert. Water is not a liquid there. It is frozen in the cold. Is it
119	believable that Mars was once warm?
125	**Red Rover**
127	Scientists wanted to know what Mars was once like. They
137	sent machines called rovers to find out. The first one landed on
149	Mars in 1997. It sent images of Mars back to Earth. It let us know
164	about the rocks and soil. These useful facts led to an answer.
176	Scientists say Mars was once warm and wet like Earth is today.

Name _____

Red Planet Plants

The rovers helped us learn about Mars. Scientists now want to send people to Mars to learn more. It would take nearly a year and a half to go there and back. This is a long way to go. People would need to bring food and water. It would be hard to go so far with enough supplies. Researchers at NASA have a solution. They want to make special plants. These

Rovers like this one conduct science experiments on Mars.

plants could live on cold and icy Mars. They could be carefully grown in a greenhouse there. The plants could grow food for researchers on Mars.

If plants are grown for food on Mars, people would have to bring less food. They could have enough supplies to stay longer if food is grown there. How is this helpful? The longer researchers stay, the more they can learn about the Red Planet.

The surface of Mars is cold, rocky, and empty. It is not full of life like Earth. However, evidence shows that Mars's climate was once like that of Earth. Research has helped us learn a lot about Mars. People might be going to Mars to learn more. Growing plants on Mars can provide food for people who are there to study the Red Planet. This could help them stay longer to learn more. Advances like these can help us truly unlock more mysteries of Mars.

Name _____

A. Reread the passage and answer the questions.

1. What are the key details in the third paragraph?

_____

_____

_____

2. How are these key details connected?

_____

_____

_____

3. What is the main idea in the fifth paragraph?

_____

_____

_____

B. Work with a partner. Read the passage aloud. Pay attention to accuracy and phrasing. Stop after one minute. Fill out the chart.

	Words Read	–	Number of Errors	=	Words Correct Score
First Read		–		=	
Second Read		–		=	

Name _____

The Rings of Saturn

The planet Saturn has many amazing rings. Saturn's rings look solid from far away. However, they are made up of billions of pieces of rock and ice. Some of these pieces are as fine as dust. Others are as big as mountains. Scientists think some of the rock and ice are pieces of an old moon. This moon may have fallen out of its orbit and crashed into Saturn.

Name of Ring	Width of Ring
Ring C	17,500 km
Ring B	25,500 km
Ring A	14,600 km

Answer the questions about the text.

1. How do you know this is expository text?

_____

2. What text features does the text include?

_____

3. What information does the chart give you?

_____

4. How does the heading help you understand the text?

_____

Name _____

Suffix	Meaning
-able	can be
-ful	full of
-ly	in a certain manner or way; like
-y	full of

A. Read each question below. Add the suffix *-able, -ful, -ly,* or *-y* to the word in the box that best answers each question. Write the new word on the line after the question. Then write the meaning of the new word. Use the information about suffixes above to help you.

rock	near	ice	true	careful	help	believe

1. How are the sidewalks after a snowfall? _____

2. What is a mountain's surface like? _____

3. What might your parents call you if you clean your room? _____

   _____

4. What do you call a story that seems real? _____

5. If one apple is almost the same as another apple, how alike are the two?

   _____

6. How do you do a task that you are asked to do with thought and detail?

   _____

7. What is the opposite of "doubtfully"? _____

Name _____

A. Read each word in the box and listen for the /âr/ or /îr/ sound. Then write the word under the correct heading.

gear	stairs	there	career
shared	pear	bear	dear
peer	careful	pair	anywhere

air as in *chair*   *are* as in *care*   *ear* as in *wear*

_____   _____   _____

_____   _____   _____

ear as in *fear*   *ere* as in *where*   *eer* as in *cheer*

_____   _____   _____

_____   _____   _____

B. Write a word with the suffix -y or -ly on the line to match the meaning of each underlined phrase.

1. My teacher speaks in a quiet way in the library. _____

2. The day was full of rain, but we still had fun. _____

3. I walked in a sad way after we lost the game. _____

4. The baby was having a mess and dropped the food. _____

5. The bus driver drives in a slow way down my street. _____

Name _____

Evidence is details and examples from a text that support a writer's ideas. This student wrote about how the author uses key details that go together to support the main idea.

Topic sentence → In "Seeing Red," the author uses key details that go together to support the main idea that scientists sent rovers to Mars to learn more about the planet. I read

Evidence → that scientists sent machines called rovers to learn about Mars. Rovers sent images of Mars back to Earth. Scientists learned about the rocks and soil on Mars. They learned that Mars was once warm and wet like

Concluding statement → Earth is today. The author uses key details that go together and support the main idea that rovers were sent to learn about Mars.

Write a paragraph about a text you read. Find text evidence to support how the author uses key details that go together to support the main idea.

Write a topic sentence: _____

_____

Cite evidence from the text: _____

_____

_____

_____

End with a concluding statement: _____

_____

Name _____

A. Read the draft model. Use questions that follow the draft to help you think about how to strengthen the topic sentence and related ideas.

Draft Model

I once saw a comet in the night sky at my brother's baseball game. The comet had a long, glowing tail. It flew across the sky and then was gone.

---

1. What is the topic of the draft model? What details could be added or rearranged to make the topic clearer?

2. In what ways could supporting details be strengthened?

3. What other details could be added to help support the topic?

B. Now revise the draft by revising sentences and adding details to create a strong topic sentence and strong supporting sentences.

_____

_____

_____

_____

_____

_____

Name _____

> | | | | |
> |---|---|---|---|
> | model | effective | example | observed |
> | identical | similar | imitate | material |

Use a word from the box to answer each question. Then use the word in a sentence.

1. If two things are impossible to tell apart, what might they be? _____

   _____

2. When making a poster, what is paper considered? _____

   _____

3. How would you describe a plan that went the way it was intended?

   _____

4. What is another word for *noticed something*? _____

   _____

5. What might be used to show what something is like? _____

   _____

6. If two things are alike, what can they be considered? _____

   _____

7. What is another word for *copy*? _____

   _____

8. What would a smaller version of a much larger building be called? _____

   _____

Name _____

Read the selection. Complete the main idea and key details graphic organizer.

```
┌─────────────────────────────────────┐
│             Main Idea               │
│                                     │
│                                     │
└─────────────────────────────────────┘
                  ↓
┌─────────────────────────────────────┐
│              Detail                 │
│                                     │
│                                     │
└─────────────────────────────────────┘
                  ↓
┌─────────────────────────────────────┐
│              Detail                 │
│                                     │
│                                     │
└─────────────────────────────────────┘
                  ↓
┌─────────────────────────────────────┐
│              Detail                 │
│                                     │
│                                     │
└─────────────────────────────────────┘
```

Name _____

Read the passage. Use the summarize strategy to find the most important ideas and details.

A Sticky Idea

Nature can inspire ideas. Take the tree frog for instance. Have
11 you ever tried to stick a piece of tape on something after it has
25 gathered dirt or dust? Take tape off of a surface and try to use it
40 again. It does not stick. The tree frog may hold the solution.

52 A tree frog has sticky pads on its feet. The stickiness of the
65 pads helps the frog to hold onto trees or rocks. Yet the pads do
79 not pick up dirt. They stay clean as the frog moves around.

91 **New Ideas**

93 The way this frog's foot works can be copied and used for
105 many purposes. It can give us ideas for other inventions.

115 For example, think about doctors and nurses at work. They
125 could reuse bandages used for patients if they stayed clean and
136 sticky. A smaller bandage used at home could also be taken off
148 and used many times.

152 Tire and car makers also have a use for what a tree frog's
165 foot can do. Material that can get a good grip and stay clean
178 could improve tire performance. It could help cars stay on the
189 road in bad weather.

193 A product like that could also make a good glue or tape. A
206 clean adhesive that lasts long would be helpful at home and at
218 school.

Name _____

Put to the Test

Researchers tested a group of tree frogs. They placed the frogs on platforms and then slanted and moved the platforms. They put dust on the frogs' feet. At first the research showed that these frogs lost their grip on the surface if they did not move. When they moved their feet, though, they were able to get back their hold.

How It Works

How do tree frogs' special feet clean themselves? Their feet produce a slimy substance called mucus. This secretion is released with

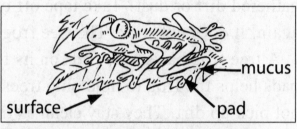

The mucus on the bottom of a frog's foot renews after every step, keeping the foot sticky and clean.

every step the frogs take. The old mucus stays behind with the dust and dirt. The new mucus helps the frogs' feet stick. This process cleans their feet as they move forward.

Tree frogs' feet also have a pattern of six-sided shapes on the bottom. The shape of the pattern is good at keeping the frogs' pads in touch with the surface they are standing on. It also helps the mucus spread across the pad.

Studying frogs' feet is just one way that people can find inspiration in nature. Ideas come from things all around us. No one knows what is coming next. What is your prediction?

Name _____

A. Reread the passage and answer the questions.

1. What are three key details in paragraphs 4, 5, and 6?

_____

_____

_____

2. How are these details connected?

_____

_____

3. Using the details, what is the main idea of the whole passage?

_____

_____

B. Work with a partner. Read the passage aloud. Pay attention to phrasing and rate. Stop after one minute. Fill out the chart.

	Words Read	–	Number of Errors	=	Words Correct Score
First Read		–		=	
Second Read		–		=	

Name _____

Against the Flow

Fish can use little energy to move in the opposite direction of flowing water. They use whirlpools to help them. Whirlpools are spinning pools of water around rocks. They pull in things around them. Fish move their bodies back and forth so they are pulled from whirlpool to whirlpool. Scientists study fish to build boats that use less energy.

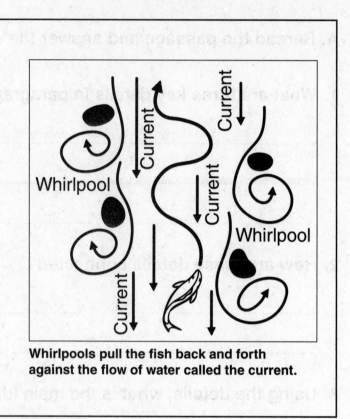

Whirlpools pull the fish back and forth against the flow of water called the current.

Answer the questions about the text.

1. How do you know this is expository text?

_____

2. What text features does the text include?

_____

3. How does the diagram help you understand the text?

_____

4. What does the caption do?

_____

Name _____

**Read each sentence below. Write the root word of the word in
bold on the line. Then write the definition of the word in bold.**

1. Its design can give us ideas for other **inventions**.

   _____

   _____

2. A product that can get a good grip and stay clean could improve tire
   performance.

   _____

   _____

3. **Researchers** tested a group of tree frogs.

   _____

   _____

4. Studying frogs' feet is just one way that people can find **inspiration**
   in nature.

   _____

   _____

5. What is your **prediction**?

   _____

   _____

Name _____

A. The prefix *pre-* means "before." The prefix *dis-* means "not." The prefix *mis-* means "bad" or "wrong." Read each set of words and circle the word that has a prefix. Write its meaning on the line.

1. problem   paper   preheat   _____

2. daily   distrust   darling   _____

3. memory   misspell   messy   _____

4. parting   pencil   preview   _____

5. mistreat   misty   mindful   _____

B. Read each sentence and underline the word that has a VCe pattern in the final syllable. Write the word on the line and circle the letters that make the pattern.

1. I think we will retake the photos. _____

2. I had to fly in an airplane last year. _____

3. When do you think our friends will arrive? _____

4. They will plan a surprise party for Mom. _____

5. The sunshine is pouring through the window. _____

Name _____

Evidence is details and examples from a text that support a writer's opinion. This student wrote about whether or not the author uses enough key details that go together to figure out the main idea, or most important point of the text.

Topic sentence → In "A Sticky Idea," the author uses key details that go together to help me figure out the main idea. In the section "How It Works," the author says that a tree frog's

Evidence → feet produce mucous. Mucous is released every time the frog takes a step. I read that the old mucous stays behind and the new mucous cleans the frog's feet as it moves forward. I can put the details together to figure out that the main idea is how the tree frog's feet clean

Concluding statement → themselves. The author gives several key details that go together and help me figure out the main idea.

Write a paragraph about a text you read. Find text evidence to support your opinion about whether or not the author uses enough key details that go together to help you figure out the main idea.

Write a topic sentence: _____

_____

Cite evidence from the text: _____

_____

_____

_____

End with a concluding statement: _____

_____

Name _____

A. Read the draft model. Use questions that follow the draft to help you think about how to strengthen the conclusion.

Draft Model

I would like to invent a ride that is similar to a falling maple tree seed. I think kids would enjoy it. Like the seeds, it would start up high. Then it would spin down and land softly.

---

1. What is the main idea of the draft model? What points support it?

2. How could the conclusion be revised to better sum up the main idea and supporting points?

3. What details could be added to give the reader something further to think about?

B. Now revise the draft by adding and rearranging details to create a strong conclusion that sums up the main idea.

_____

_____

_____

_____

_____

_____

Name _____

| boomed | agreeable | descendants | emigration |
| appreciate | pioneers | vehicles | transportation |

Finish each sentence using the vocabulary word provided.

1. **(boomed)** Because of its good location, _____

   _____

2. **(appreciate)** It is important _____

   _____

3. **(agreeable)** During the springtime, _____

   _____

4. **(pioneers)** People in the 19th century _____

   _____

5. **(descendants)** My family's _____

   _____

6. **(vehicles)** The best way to travel long distances _____

   _____

7. **(emigration)** The history of the United States _____

   _____

8. **(transportation)** If I want to go to the movies, _____

   _____

Name _____

Read the selection. Complete the sequence graphic organizer.

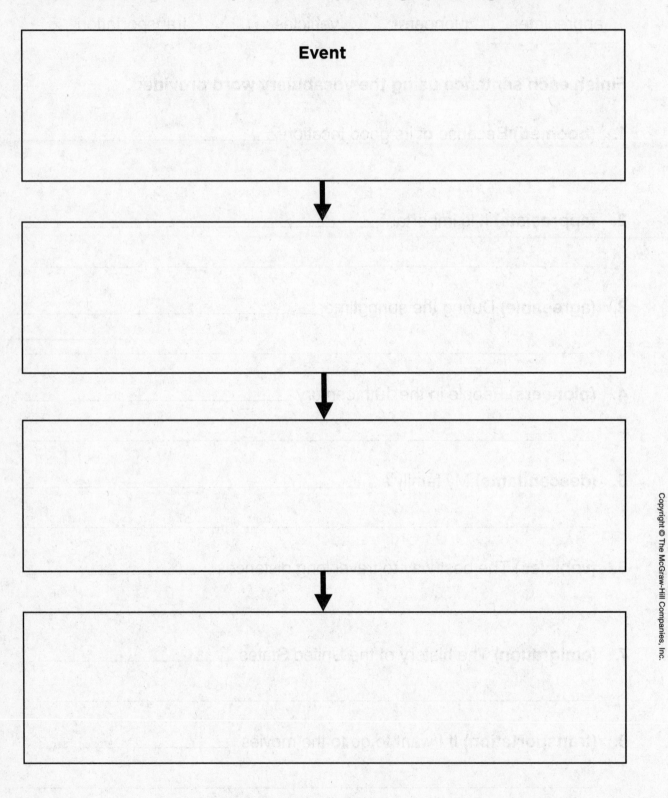

Event

Name _____

Read the passage. Use the summarize strategy to be sure you understand the text.

Mississippi Steamboats

	What if you want something sent from far away? The goods
11	will travel by truck or plane. But what did people do before
23	trucks and planes? How did things travel from far away? Two
34	hundred years ago, goods traveled on the Mississippi River.
43	Steamboats carried them.

46	**What Is a Steamboat?**

50	A steamboat is any boat powered by steam. Water is boiled and
62	turned into steam. The steam creates a force. This force is used
74	to power an engine. Steamboats often had a wheel in the back.
86	The engine would turn the wheel. This moved the steamboat
96	forward. Captains steered the steamboats from a little house
105	on the roof of the cabin. They had to be watchful of objects in
119	the river.

121	**Shreve Adapts the Steamboat**

125	John Fitch made the first successful steamboat. But it could
135	only float in deep water. The Mississippi was not deep. This
146	problem was fixable though. Henry Shreve adapted the steamboat
155	for the Mississippi River. First, Shreve made the steamboats able
165	to float in shallow water. Next, he used a high-pressure steam
176	engine. This made the steamboat faster. Finally, he added a
186	tall upper deck. Shreve's steamboat was the model for all other
197	Mississippi steamboats.

Name _____

The Golden Age of Steamboats

When steamboats first began to work the Mississippi, they were slow. Then steamboats got faster. People used them more. In 1834 there were about two hundred packets on the river. Twenty years later, there were about 1,000. The packet became the best way to travel the Mississippi for the next fifty years.

"Packet"-style steamboats were common on the Mississippi in the 19th century.

Mark Twain wrote a book called *Life on the Mississippi*. It was about his days as a steamboat captain. Sometimes Twain made steamboat travel sound nice. Yet life on a steamboat could be hard. If the captain was careless, it could be a risky way to travel. The captain had to be careful on moonless nights when it was hard to see.

The End of an Era

At first, steamboats were all over the Mississippi River. Then the railroad came along. Trains were much faster. Trains became the most acceptable way to travel. Finally, by 1920, the steamboat had all but died out. It was the end of the steamboat era.

A Steamboat for Every Occasion

There were different types of steamboats. Towboats pushed barges on the river. Boats called "packets" carried goods and people. There were even showboats, which people used to hold parties.

Currier & Ives (American printing firm, 1834–1907)/ Historicus, Inc/Library of Congress Prints and Photographs Division [LC-USZC2-2523]

Name _____

A. Reread the passage and answer the questions.

1. Who made the first successful steamboat?

_____

2. What was the first thing Henry Shreve did to adapt the steamboat for use on the Mississippi?

_____

_____

3. What happened after steamboats got faster?

_____

_____

4. What happened after railroads became the most acceptable way to travel?

_____

_____

B. Work with a partner. Read the passage aloud. Pay attention to accuracy and phrasing. Stop after one minute. Fill out the chart.

	Words Read	–	Number of Errors	=	Words Correct Score
First Read		–		=	
Second Read		–		=	

Name _____

The End of the Pony Express

On October 24, 1861, after nineteen months of service, the Pony Express came to an end. On that day the Pacific Telegraph Line was completed. Important information that had to be sent in letters could now be sent through a wire. News from one side of the continent could reach the other in seconds. Men no longer needed to ride horses over the dangerous 2,000-mile trail to deliver letters. But Americans would never forget the service these men provided for the country.

How Telegraphs Work

Tetra Images/Corbis

A telegraph operator taps out a message using Morse code, a system of dashes and dots. This message is sent as an electronic signal through a wire. The person on the other end receives the signal and decodes the message.

Answer the questions about the text.

1. **How can you tell that this is an informational text?**

_____

2. **What text features are included?**

_____

3. **How does the sidebar help you understand the text?**

_____

_____

_____

Name _____

Read each sentence below. Underline the suffix of the word in bold and write the word's definition on the line.

1. Captains steered the steamboats from a little house on the roof of the cabin. They had to be **watchful** of objects in the river.

   _____

   _____

2. John Fitch made the first **successful** steamboat.

   _____

   _____

3. The Mississippi was not deep. This problem was **fixable** though.

   _____

   _____

4. The captain had to be careful on **moonless** nights when it was hard to see.

   _____

   _____

5. Trains became the most **acceptable** way to travel.

   _____

   _____

Name _____

A. Read each word in the box. Sort the words by writing each under the correct heading.

found	clown	down	enjoy
join	toys	noise	moist
joyful	loud	pounce	prowl

oy as in **boy**   **ou** as in **house**

_____   _____

_____   _____

_____   _____

oi as in **boil**   **ow** as in **cow**

_____   _____

_____   _____

B. The prefixes *un-*, *dis-*, and *non-* mean "not" or "the opposite of." Read each word pair. Circle the word that has a prefix. Write its meaning on the line.

1. disagree   dishes   _____

2. uncle   unknown   _____

3. nonfiction   notebook   _____

4. understand   unhappy   _____

5. daily   distrust   _____

Name _____

Evidence is details and examples from a text that support a writer's ideas. This student wrote about how the author uses signal words to show the sequence of important events in a text.

Topic sentence → In "Mississippi Steamboats," the author uses signal words to tell the history of steamboats in time order. I read that steamboats could not float in the

Evidence → Mississippi River because the water was not deep. First, Henry Shreve fixed the steamboats. Next, he used a steam engine so the boat would go faster. Finally, the author says that Shreve added an upper deck. Henry Shreve fixed the problem. The author

Concluding statement → tells the history of the Mississippi steamboats in time order using words like *first, next,* and *finally.*

Write a paragraph about a story you read. Find text evidence to show how the author uses signal words to put important events in time order. Use text evidence to support your ideas.

Write a topic sentence: _____

_____

Cite evidence from the text: _____

_____

_____

End with a concluding statement: _____

_____

Name _____

A. Read the draft model. Use the questions that follow the draft to help you think about formal and informal voice.

Draft Model

Studying history is super important. You can get a feel for what it was like in the past. History can also teach you a lot of stuff. It can show you about how our country came to be or why we do things the way we do today.

---

1. Who might the writer be addressing in this model?

2. What word can be used to replace the word "super" in the first sentence?

3. What word can be used to replace the word "stuff" in the third sentence?

4. How can you make the wording in the last sentence sound more formal?

B. Now revise the draft by adding clues to show the writer's use of formal or informal voice.

_____

_____

_____

_____

_____

_____

Name _____

| flavorful | luscious | expect | aroma |
| variety | healthful | graceful | interrupted |

Finish each sentence using the vocabulary word provided.

1. **(expect)** Each autumn _____

_____ .

2. **(flavorful)** I think the new recipe _____

_____ .

3. **(aroma)** My mother's perfume _____

_____ .

4. **(luscious)** It's the time of year when our garden _____

_____ .

5. **(graceful)** After many years of swimming lessons, _____

_____ .

6. **(interrupted)** I started to tell her the roof was leaking, ____

_____ .

7. **(variety)** My brother eats the same cereal every morning, ____

_____ .

8. **(healthful)** As a snack, fruit is _____

_____ .

Name _____

Read the selection. Complete the point of view graphic organizer.

Details

↓

Point of View

Name _____

Read the passage. Use the ask and answer questions strategy to find details and answer questions.

The Turtle and the Box of Riches

	Long ago there was a young fisherman's helper sitting on a
11	dock. As he waited for his boat to head out for the day, he heard
26	a group of children laughing under the dock. He peeked down
37	and saw them teasing and pushing a small turtle.
46	"Leave that turtle alone!" the boy shouted and jumped down.
56	The children quickly ran away. The boy picked up the turtle.
67	"Thank you," the turtle said.
72	The boy jumped. "You can talk?"
78	"Yes," the turtle said. "I am a very powerful turtle in my
90	land. Your act was an inspiration. I want to reward you for your
103	kindness. Go to sleep tonight, and when you wake up, you will be
116	in a wonderful place."
120	The turtle swam out to sea. The boy went to bed that night in
134	disbelief. Yet, the next morning he woke up in a beautiful palace.
146	"Welcome to our home under the sea," the turtle greeted him.
157	The turtle took the boy through the underwater palace. Large
167	windows showed many types of fish and plant life. Gold walls
178	and mirrored ceilings shined brightly. The boy met all of the
189	friendly turtles that lived in the palace. Later that day, they had a
202	big feast, and the boy ate more than he had ever eaten before.

Name _____

As night came the boy asked to return to his home.

"Thank you so much for all you have shown and given me," he said. "I have a lot of admiration for your home, but I must return to my home before morning. I have to work on a fishing boat and cannot afford to miss a day's pay."

"I understand," the turtle said calmly. "Take a rest after your big meal, my friend. When you wake up, you will be back in your bed. But before you go, take this box."

The turtle handed the boy a box with two drawers. Then he gave him a key. He told him to open the box at home.

"Take this key," he said. "Use it to open one of the drawers—either one—but do not ever open the other. You must promise."

The box had one key and two drawers.

The boy promised and fell asleep on some pillows. When he woke up, he was in his bedroom. There was the box sitting next to him. He took the key and opened the top drawer. It was filled with gold and jewels! The boy was rich and knew he wouldn't have to work again.

The boy was filled with appreciation but could not help but wonder about the second drawer. What if he had opened it first? Might he have found even greater riches? He opened the drawer but it was empty. Quickly he opened the first drawer again. The gold and jewels had turned to dust. Instead of a rich man he was just a fisherman's helper once more.

Name _____

A. Reread the passage and answer the questions.

1. What do the first seven lines of the passage tell you about how the narrator thinks about the fisherman's helper?

_____

_____

_____

2. Do you think the narrator approves of what the fisherman's helper does? Use text evidence to support your answer.

_____

_____

_____

3. What is the narrator's point of view about the fisherman's helper at the end of the passage? Does the narrator still think the same as at the beginning of the passage?

_____

_____

_____

_____

B. Work with a partner. Read the passage aloud. Pay attention to expression. Stop after one minute. Fill out the chart.

	Words Read	–	Number of Errors	=	Words Correct Score
First Read		–		=	
Second Read		–		=	

Name _____

Kyoto Frog and Osaka Frog

Two frogs lived in Japan. One frog was from Kyoto. The other was from Osaka. Each frog set out to see the other's town. They met halfway between Osaka and Kyoto. Both were very tired. Neither knew if he could go on. Then Osaka Frog had an idea.

"We should help each other stand on our hind legs. That way we can look out at the towns we want to visit. Then we'll know if we really want to keep walking," Osaka Frog said. Each frog faced the town he wished to see. Then each pushed the other up on his hind legs. But when they did this, their underbellies faced the town they wanted to go to and their eyes faced back home.

"Kyoto looks just like Osaka!" said Osaka Frog.

"And Osaka looks just like Kyoto!" said Kyoto Frog.

Each decided to go home rather than travel to a town that looked exactly like home. So each went home, not knowing that Kyoto and Osaka were as different as two cities could be.

Answer the questions about the text.

1. How do you know this is a folktale?

_____

2. What problem do the frogs have to solve?

_____

_____

3. What do you think is the message or lesson of this folktale?

_____

Copyright © The McGraw-Hill Companies, Inc.

Name _____

Read each sentence below. Write the root word of the word in bold on the line. Then write the definition of the word in bold.

1. I am a very **powerful** turtle in my land.

_____

2. Your act was an **inspiration**.

_____

3. I want to reward you for your **kindness**.

_____

4. I have a lot of **admiration** for your home, but I must return to my home before morning.

_____

5. The boy was filled with **appreciation** but could not help but wonder about the second drawer.

_____

Name _____

A. Read each word in the box. Sort the words by writing each under the correct heading.

true	booth	look	glue
shook	tube	grew	should
would	spoon	flew	tune

oo as in *moon*

_____

_____

ew as in *chew*

_____

_____

u_e as in *rude*

_____

_____

ue as in *due*

_____

_____

oo as in *book*

_____

_____

ou as in *could*

_____

_____

B. Related words have a common root or base word. Read each set of words. Circle the related words.

1. metal   metallic   melted

2. company   counting   companion

3. able   action   actor

4. telephone   totally   television

5. reality   real   railroad

Name _____

Evidence is details and examples from a text that support a writer's ideas. The student who wrote the paragraph below found text evidence that shows how the author uses details about events and other characters to share what the narrator thinks about the fisherman's helper.

Topic sentence →   In "The Turtle and the Box of Riches," the author uses what the boy and the turtle do and say to share the narrator's point of view. At the beginning of

Evidence → the story, fisherman's helper saves the turtle. The narrator thinks helping animals is important. Then the turtle rewards the boy. The narrator thinks that acts of kindness should be rewarded. I read that at the end of the story, the narrator thinks the boy is still good, but he makes a mistake. The author

Concluding statement → uses what the boy does to show that the narrator thinks he is a good person. I agree with the narrator because the boy helped the turtle.

Write about a folktale you have read. Find text evidence to show how the author uses details to share the narrator's point of view.

Write a topic sentence: _____

_____

Cite evidence from the text: _____

_____

_____

_____

End with a concluding statement: _____

_____

Name _____

A. Read the draft model. Use the questions that follow the draft to help you think about using your voice to show feelings.

Draft Model

On Saturday mornings, I play soccer with my friend Lauren. We go to the fields at the high school. Lauren plays soccer on a neighborhood team. I do not play soccer for any team.

---

1. How do you feel about playing soccer?

2. How did you choose the high school for a place to play soccer?

3. What do you like about being able to play soccer with your friend Lauren?

4. Is there anything you wish were different about the time you spend with your friend?

B. Now revise the draft by adding your voice to show how you feel about participating in this activity.

_____

_____

_____

_____

_____

Name _____

achievement	attention	confidence	apologized
talents	audience	realized	embarrassed

Use the context clues in each sentence to help you decide which vocabulary word fits best in the blank.

Madeleine had many _____, such as singing and dancing. However, she liked acting the most. There was nothing she enjoyed more than being on stage in front of an _____ and performing in a play. If all went well, the lead role in the school play would surely be hers. Getting the part would be a great _____ .

On the day of the audition, Madeleine was ready. She knew her lines by heart and had a lot of _____ that she would get the lead role.

"I'm so excited!" said her best friend, Helen. "I can't wait to be in the play!"

"I want the lead role," said Madeleine. She got up on stage for the audition. Somehow, she couldn't remember her lines! Madeleine's face turned red, she started sweating, and she felt more _____ than ever before. She said she was sorry and _____ to her teacher. "I don't remember my lines," said Madeleine. She quickly walked off the stage.

"What's the matter?" asked Helen.

"I forgot my lines!" said Madeleine. "Now I won't be in the play! I wish no one had been watching me or paying _____ at all."

"Everyone knows you're talented," said Helen. "You just made one mistake. It's okay. I think that you will still be in the play no matter what."

Madeleine understood what Helen meant. She _____ it would be fun to be on stage with her best friend Helen, even if she didn't get the lead role.

Name _____

Read the selection. Complete the point of view graphic organizer.

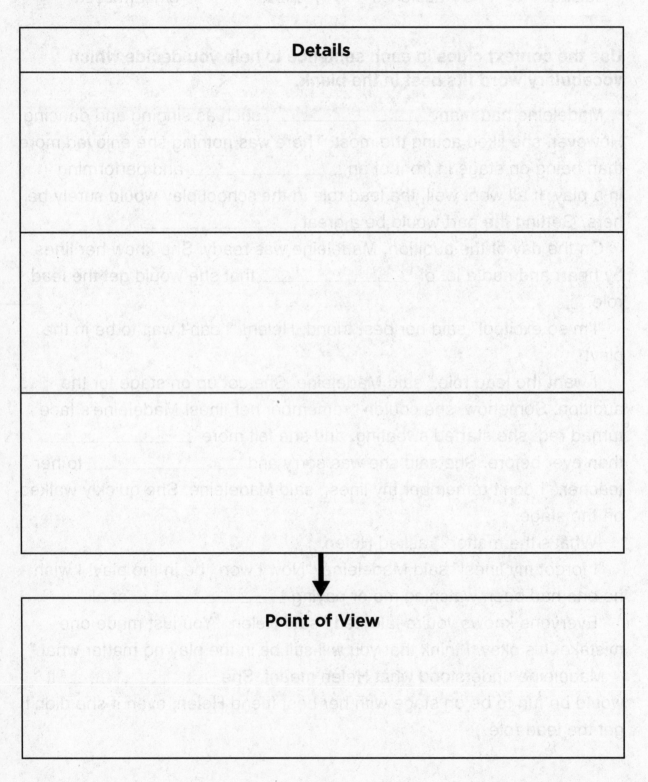

Details

↓

Point of View

Name _____

Read the passage. Use the ask and answer questions strategy to tell about the most important details of the passage.

Painting From Memory

	Few people know of Damyang, South Korea, but I think it is
12	impossible to find a place more beautiful. It is known for its bamboo
25	forests. When I was younger, I spent much time in the forests
37	painting pictures of the bamboo. Painting is one of my talents.
48	I lived in Damyang until last year when my family moved to
60	New York. My mother, a scientist, was asked to come work here.
72	"There are no bamboo forests in New York," I said. "There is
84	nothing to paint in New York."
90	"Bae," she said, "that is nonsense. You will find many things
101	to see and paint there. You will see."
109	I was unsure. "But I will miss home," I said.
119	"Then you must paint pictures of your favorite places," she
129	said. "They will make you feel at home even in New York."
141	So when we moved, I brought my forest paintings with me.
152	New York was not easy at first, because I knew no one and spoke
166	only imperfect English. Yet I didn't feel homesick when I looked at
178	my paintings of home. I soon found friends at school, too. Like me,
191	they were artists, and we now paint in a group after school.
203	Last month someone moved into the apartment next to my
213	family's. "Come, Bae," said my mother. "Let's welcome our
222	neighbor." We crossed the hall and knocked on the door. An old
234	woman who looked kind yet unhappy answered.

Name _____

"We are your new neighbors," my mother said to her. "I am Hana and this is my son, Bae."

The woman smiled. "I am Varvara. Please come in."

We learned that Varvara had moved from Vyborg, Russia, to be closer to her daughter. Still, she was sad to leave her home.

New York was not easy at first. My paintings helped me feel better though.

"I am so homesick it is unbearable," Varvara said. She laughed, but I could tell she was sad. Varvara told us so much about Vyborg. I could picture her home in my head.

When I came home from school the next day, an ambulance was leaving our building, and I asked my mother why.

"It's Varvara. She misses her home so much that she has become ill. I hope she can get used to living here. Try not to worry."

I had to do something for Varvara. I had been in her situation before. I had missed my home so much it hurt. But at least I had my paintings of home. She didn't even have that. Unless…

A few days later I heard Varvara on the stairs. I cracked the door to see her. She looked better but still sad. When she got to her door she gasped. Propped against the door was my gift to her: a painting of Vyborg. I had painted it from her memories.

I closed the door as she began to cry. At first I was worried that she didn't like the painting. But later she told me that those were tears of joy. I knew just how she felt.

Name _____

A. Reread the passage and answer the questions.

1. What is Bae's point of view in the third paragraph about moving to New York?

_____

_____

2. How have Bae's feelings about moving to New York changed in the eighth paragraph?

_____

_____

3. Give one detail from the passage that helps you figure out why Bae wants to help Varvara.

_____

_____

_____

B. Work with a partner. Read the passage aloud. Pay attention to phrasing. Stop after one minute. Fill out the chart.

	Words Read	–	Number of Errors	=	Words Correct Score
First Read		–		=	
Second Read		–		=	

Name _____

Class by the Pond

Fumiko's class was about to have a quiz about the life cycle of a frog. She was surprised that her class was so worried. She knew lots about frogs since she often watched them by the school pond. Then she had an idea.

"Can we have class by the pond tomorrow?" Fumiko asked as she pointed out the window.

"Why do you ask?" replied Ms. McNally.

"The frog eggs are starting to hatch. Maybe going to the pond and studying the tadpoles will help us learn more about them," Fumiko said.

Answer the questions about the text.

1. How do you know this is realistic fiction?

_____

2. Why do you think the author uses dialogue?

_____

3. What text feature is included? How does it help show that the text is realistic fiction?

_____

Name _____

Add the prefix _pre-_, _un-_, _im-_, or _non-_ to the words in the box below. Then complete the sentences with the new words.

> _____ heat   _____ sure   _____ possible
>
> _____ bearable   _____ sense   _____ perfect

1. Without my coat on, I find the cold weather is _____.

2. He was _____ of how to answer the question because he did not study.

3. This riddle is _____! I don't understand it at all.

4. Some people said training an elephant was _____, but she said that it could be done.

5. I will _____ the oven before baking the pie.

6. The beautiful diamond had a small scratch on it that made it

   _____.

Name _____

A. Read each sentence below. Circle the word that has the correct plural spelling.

1. Last summer my family visited five (states, stateses).

2. How many (lunchs, lunches) should we make for the field trip?

3. After the forest fire, the trees were reduced to (ashes, ashs).

4. We need several (trays, trayes) to clear the tables.

5. People were surprised that the (twines, twins) looked so different.

6. My puppy grew two more (inchs, inches) since his last vet visit.

B. Read each word in bold. Circle the letter that shows the word correctly divided into syllables. Then underline each vowel team in the correctly divided word.

1. teacher   **a.** teach / er   **b.** te / acher

2. explain   **a.** expl / ain   **b.** ex / plain

3. railroad   **a.** rail / road   **b.** ra / il / road

4. reaches   **a.** re / aches   **b.** reach / es

5. seeing   **a.** see / ing   **b.** se / eing

Name _____

Evidence is details and examples from a text that support a writer's opinion. This student wrote an opinion about whether or not the author gives enough details about events and other characters in the story to figure out Bae's point of view.

Topic sentence →   In "Painting from Memory," the author gives enough details about Bae for me to figure out that he wants to help Varvara. At the beginning of the story,

Evidence → Bae is homesick because his family moves to New York. Painting helps him feel better. Then a new neighbor moves in. Varvara is so homesick. I read that Bae was in her situation before. So he paints a

Concluding statement → picture for Varvara. The author gives details about Bae and it helps me figure out his point of view about Varvara and how he thinks he can help.

Write your opinion about a story you read. Find text evidence to support your opinion about whether or not the author gives enough details about events and other characters in the story to figure out the narrator's point of view.

Write a topic sentence: _____

_____

Cite evidence from the text: _____

_____

_____

_____

End with a concluding statement: _____

_____

Name _____

A. Read the draft model. Use the questions that follow the draft to help you think about how dialogue can help develop characters.

Draft Model

My little brother Henry was upset. He was studying for a math test but was having trouble with subtraction. He asked if I could help him.

---

1. How did you know that your brother was upset? Did he say something?

2. What was your brother feeling when he explained his problem?

3. How would you reply when your brother asked you for a favor? What would you say?

4. How could dialogue better help someone understand what is going on in the story?

B. Now revise the draft by adding dialogue to show the characters' thoughts, feelings, and actions in the story.

_____

_____

_____

_____

_____

_____

Name _____

excellent	prefer	environment	shelter
alert	protection	related	competition

Finish each sentence using the vocabulary word provided.

1. **(environment)** A desert _____

   _____.

2. **(prefer)** When it comes to reading books, _____

   _____.

3. **(competition)** Those are the two best soccer teams, _____

   _____.

4. **(excellent)** She lived by the beach her whole life _____

   _____.

5. **(related)** Since my sister and I look exactly alike, _____

   _____.

6. **(protection)** A turtle has a hard shell _____

   _____.

7. **(shelter)** My father and I built a doghouse _____

   _____.

8. **(alert)** The town has a loud siren _____

   _____.

Name _____

Read the selection. Complete the compare and contrast graphic organizer.

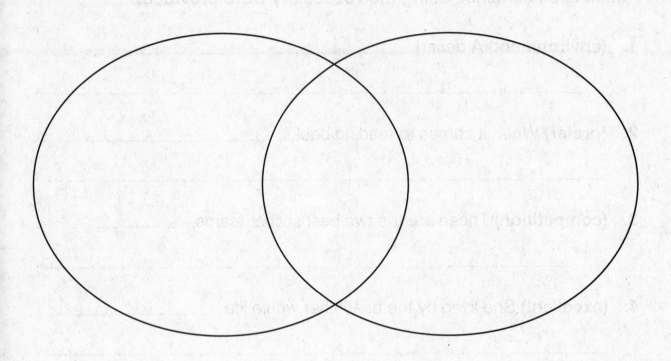

Name _____

Read the passage. Use the reread strategy to be sure you understand what you read.

Adaptations: Grizzly and Polar Bears

10	Every animal has adaptations. These are special ways that a body works or is made. Not all birds eat the same things. Their
23	beaks have different shapes. Some fish that live at the bottom of
35	the ocean glow in the dark. Mammals live all over the world, so
48	they need to have different skills and body shapes. Giraffes have
59	long tongues. They use them to pull leaves off the tops of trees.
72	Jackrabbits have wide feet to run across sand.
80	These things help animals be as effective as they can be. This
92	means that they can do the best job possible of finding food and
105	raising offspring. Adaptations are very important for keeping all
114	animals alive and able to reproduce, or have offspring.
123	**Similarities**
124	Mammals have adapted to live in different parts of the
134	world. Bears live all over the world. Grizzly bears live in North
146	America. Polar bears live inside the Arctic Circle. In many ways
157	they are the same. They are very large animals. They can weigh
169	more than 1,500 pounds. Both kinds of bears have toes with
180	claws they cannot retract. This means bears cannot pull their
190	claws inside. They can stand on their hind legs. They can even
202	sit up, as if they were sitting in a chair! And all bears have
216	rounded ears.

Name _____

Differences

Grizzly bears and polar bears have adapted to conditions in the different places they live. Polar bears' fur is white. They can blend in with the ice and snow in the Arctic Circle. They can sneak up on prey without being seen. They also have a layer of blubber, or fat, over four inches thick. This helps keep them warm even though the air temperature can be −80°F. Their paws have fur on the bottom. This protects them from the ice and snow.

Grizzly bears do not live in the ice and snow. Their fur is brown. This helps them blend in with the trees and rocks in their environment, or where they live. Their claws are longer than a polar bear's. Polar bears eat only meat. Grizzlies are omnivorous. They are just as happy eating fish as they are eating berries. They use their claws to catch fish. They also use them to dig in the ground for roots or

A grizzly and a polar bear in relation to a person.

insects. These bears also have a large hump of muscle over their shoulders. This makes their front legs very strong. It also helps them run quickly in order to catch prey.

Bears are only one kind of animal, and as you can see, where they live greatly affects what they are like. Adaptations are very important to bears, and they are important to every other kind of animal. Adaptations are what make each kind of bear unique.

Name _____

A. Reread the passage and answer the questions.

1. In the third paragraph, how does the author compare the two kinds of bears?

_____

_____

_____

2. In the fifth paragraph, how does the author contrast what the two kinds of bears eat?

_____

_____

_____

3. What are some of the signal words the author uses in the text to compare and contrast?

_____

_____

_____

B. Work with a partner. Read the passage aloud. Pay attention to intonation. Stop after one minute. Fill out the chart.

	Words Read	–	Number of Errors	=	Words Correct Score
First Read		–		=	
Second Read		–		=	

Name _____

The Monarch Migrations

Monarch butterflies live all over the United States. They migrate south each fall to warmer climates. Some fly all the way from Canada to Mexico. Monarchs migrate to adapt to changing temperatures. In the fall, temperatures in the north get cooler, and there are fewer flowers on plants. Monarchs cannot survive very cold winter weather and need flowering plants for food. They move to warm areas in the south where there is food.

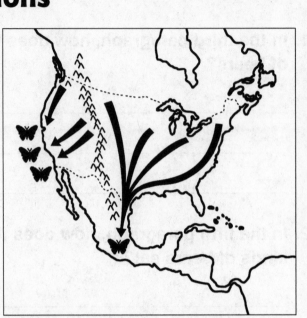

Monarch butterflies west of the Rocky Mountains fly south to California. Those east of the Rocky Mountains fly south to Mexico.

Answer the questions about the text.

1. How do you know this is expository text?

_____

2. How do the text features help the reader understand the text?

_____

_____

3. Why do monarchs migrate?

_____

Name _____

**Read each passage below. Underline the sentence clues that
help you figure out the meaning of each word in bold. On the
line, write the meaning of the word in bold.**

1. Every animal has **adaptations**. These are special ways that its body works
   or is made.

   _____

2. Adaptations are very important for keeping all animals alive and able to
   reproduce, or have offspring.

   _____

3. Both kinds of bears have toes with claws they cannot **retract**. This means
   bears cannot pull their claws inside.

   _____

4. They also have a layer of **blubber**, or fat, over four inches thick.

   _____

5. This helps them blend in with the trees and rocks in their **environment**, or
   where they live.

   _____

6. Grizzlies are **omnivorous**. They are just as happy eating fish as they are
   eating berries.

   _____

Name _____

A. Read each word in the box and listen for the vowel sound. Then write each word under the correct heading.

chalk	halt	small	crawl
thought	stalk	brought	lawn
caused	malt	halls	paused

aw as in *straw*   *alt* as in *salt*   *all* as in *ball*

_____   _____   _____

_____   _____   _____

au as in *haul*   *alk* as in *walk*   *ough* as in *bought*

_____   _____   _____

_____   _____   _____

B. Read each sentence and underline the word with the root *graph* or *aud*. Then write the word on the line and circle the root.

1. The president's autograph is very valuable. _____

2. The audience clapped after the great performance. _____

3. I read a biography about a famous astronaut. _____

4. She had a great audition and won the lead role. _____

5. I read a graphic novel about a family from outer space. _____

Name _____

Evidence is details and examples from a text that support a writer's opinion. This student wrote about whether or not the author's use of an illustration and a caption helps him understand more about grizzly bears and polar bears.

Topic sentence → In "Adaptations: Grizzly and Polar Bears," the author uses an illustration to help me understand more about grizzly bears and polar bears. In the

Evidence → section "Differences," the author uses an illustration to compare the sizes of a grizzly bear, a polar bear, and a person. The caption gives information about

Concluding statement → what is in the illustration. The author's use of the illustration and caption helps me understand more about how big grizzly and polar bears are in relation to a person and to each other.

Write a paragraph about a text you read. Find text evidence to support your opinion about the author's use of text features.

Write a topic sentence: _____

_____

Cite evidence from the text: _____

_____

_____

_____

End with a concluding statement: _____

_____

Name _____

A. Read the draft model. Use the questions that follow the draft to help you think about how you can grab the reader's attention with a strong opening.

Draft Model

A flying squirrel is a special type of squirrel. Flying squirrels move from tree to tree through the air. One squirrel's flight was 100 yards long.

---

1. How could you replace the first sentence with an interesting question that grabs the reader's attention?

2. How do flying squirrels move through the air?

3. What else is 100 yards long?

B. Now revise the draft by adding interesting questions and fascinating facts to make the reader want to read more.

_____

_____

_____

_____

_____

_____

Name _____

passenger	launched	direction	flight
impossible	popular	controlled	motion

Use a word from the box to answer each question. Then use the word in a sentence.

1. What word might describe a famous actor? _____

   _____

2. What do you call a person who rides the bus? _____

   _____

3. What is another word for *movement*? _____

   _____

4. What word describes something that cannot be done? _____

   _____

5. What did the pilot do when he flew the plane? _____

   _____

6. What is another word for *the line something moves along*? _____

   _____

7. What is another word for *put something into motion*? _____

   _____

8. Which word describes the movement of a bird through the air? _____

   _____

Name _____

Read the selection. Complete the cause and effect graphic organizer.

Cause		Effect
First	→	
Next	→	
Then	→	
Finally	→	

Name _____

Read the passage. Use the reread strategy to be sure you understand what you read.

History of Human Flight

Wanting to Fly Like Birds

5	Humans have always wanted to fly. But it took a long time
17	for them to learn how to do it. At first, they tried to copy birds.
32	They made wings out of wood. They attached the wings to their
44	arms and tried to fly. But birds and humans do not have the
57	same muscles. So the wings did not work.
65	The first big step toward human flight was the kite. The kite
77	was first made in China in 400 B.C. Some used kites for fun.
90	Others used them to test the weather. Some people wanted to
101	make flying objects that could carry people. So they made
111	balloons and gliders.

114 Hot Air Balloons

117	The first hot air balloon was a silk bag. The bag was filled with
131	smoke from a fire. The hot air made the balloon lighter than the air
145	around it. Because of this, the bag rose into the sky. People attached
158	a basket to the bag. Soon, they began to use it to travel.

171 Gliders

172	The next big step in human flight was the glider. A glider does
185	not float like a balloon. It falls to earth. But it falls so slowly that
200	it stays in the air a long time. Gliders are easier to control than
214	balloons. With gliders people could fly where they wanted.

Name _____

Several inventors helped improve the glider. George Cayley made a new wing shape. He also wanted to make the glider more stable. That's why he added a tail. Otto Lilienthal made a glider that could fly far. Sam Langley focused on ways to power the flight. He put an engine on the glider.

Really Flying

Balloons and gliders made it possible for people to fly. But they did not let people travel very far. Octave Chanute studied all of the texts he could find about human flight. He wrote it all in a book. Two brothers from Ohio read the book. Their names were Wilbur and Orville Wright. Octave's book convinced them that they could make a flying machine.

The Wright brothers' first "Flyer."

U.S. Air Force

The Wright brothers were great thinkers. First they did tests with balloons and kites. Then they learned about wind. They made a glider that worked well in any type of wind. Then they worked on an engine. It had to be strong. After five years of study, they used all their knowledge to make a "Flyer." At 10:35 A.M. on December 17, 1903, the Wright brothers tested their new Flyer. It worked! Orville Wright flew 120 feet in twelve seconds. Humans had learned to fly at last!

Name _____

A. Reread the passage and answer the questions.

1. When people made wings out of wood, why did they not work?

_____

_____

2. According to paragraph 2, why did people make balloons and gliders?

_____

_____

3. According to the section "Hot Air Balloons," what caused the silk bags to rise into the sky?

_____

_____

4. What was the effect of the Wright brothers reading Octave Chanute's book?

_____

_____

B. Work with a partner. Read the passage aloud. Pay attention to accuracy and phrasing. Stop after one minute. Fill out the chart.

	Words Read	–	Number of Errors	=	Words Correct Score
First Read		–		=	
Second Read		–		=	

Name _____

How Rockets Move

A rocket is filled with fuel. When the fuel burns, gas leaves the back of the rocket. This gas moves at a very high speed. It has a lot of force. The rocket then moves forward using a basic law of nature. This law says that every action has an equal and opposite reaction. This means that the force of the moving gas has an opposite reaction. When the gas leaves the back of the rocket, it pushes the rocket in the opposite direction. This makes the rocket move forward at a very high speed.

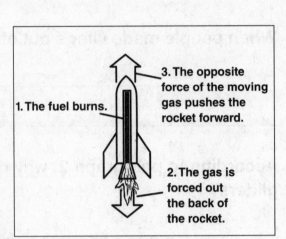

1. The fuel burns.

2. The gas is forced out the back of the rocket.

3. The opposite force of the moving gas pushes the rocket forward.

Answer the questions about the text.

1. What topic does this expository text tell about?

_____

2. What text feature does this text include?

_____

3. How does the text feature help you understand the text?

_____

Name _____

Read each passage below. Use other words in the passage to help you figure out the correct meaning of each multiple-meaning word in bold. On the line, write the correct meaning of the word in bold.

1. Humans have always wanted to **fly**. But it took a long time for them to learn how to do it. At first, they tried to copy birds.

   fly: _____

2. The kite was first made in China in 400 B.C. Some used kites for fun. Others used them to **test** the weather.

   test: _____

3. The hot air made the balloon lighter than the air. Because of this, the bag **rose** into the sky.

   rose: _____

4. Sam Langley focused on ways to **power** the flight. He put an engine on the glider.

   power: _____

5. Then they learned about **wind**. They made a glider that worked well in any type of wind.

   wind: _____

6. At 10:35 A.M. on December 17, 1903, the Wright brothers tested their new Flyer. It **worked**!

   worked: _____

Name _____

A. Circle the correct homophone to complete each sentence. Write the word on the line.

1. I think _____ report was very interesting.

    your   you're

2. We slowly _____ the canoe down the river.

    road   rowed

3. Do you think _____ going to be here on time?

    their   they're

4. I found the missing _____ of the jigsaw puzzle.

    piece   peace

5. I plan to buy the game once it goes on _____.

    sail   sale

B. Read the words in each row. Underline the word that has an r-controlled vowel syllable. Then circle the two letters that make the r-controlled vowel sound.

1. people   really   person

2. sharpen   slowing   safety

3. willow   working   waiting

4. horses   homemade   hopeful

5. sudden   sprouting   surprise

Name _____

Evidence is details and examples from a text that support a writer's opinion. This student wrote an opinion about how well the author uses causes and effects to show events in time order.

Topic sentence → In "History of Human Flight," the author uses causes and effects to show the history of flight in time order. The author writes that the first big

Evidence → step toward human flight was the kite. Because some people wanted to fly, they made balloons and gliders. People rode in hot air balloons, but they were hard to control. As a result, people invented gliders. Then Sam Langley put an engine on a glider.

Concluding statement → Finally, Orville Wright flew. The author does a good job using causes and effects to show the time order of how humans learned to fly.

Write your opinion about a story you read. Find text evidence to support your opinion of how the author uses causes and effects to show events in time order.

Write a topic sentence: _____

Cite evidence from the text: _____

_____

_____

_____

End with a concluding statement: _____

_____

Name _____

A. Read the draft model. Use the questions that follow the draft to help you think about how you can use a strong conclusion.

> # Draft Model
>
> I like helicopters. They can fly in any direction. They can go fast or slow and land almost anywhere. They can be used to rescue people, to help fight forest fires, or to prevent crimes.

1. What is the main idea? Are helicopters the writer's favorite flying machine?

2. What directions can a helicopter fly in?

3. What kinds of birds are helicopters like?

4. What conclusion could be added to restate the main idea?

B. Now revise the draft by adding a strong conclusion that retells the main idea.

_____

_____

_____

_____

_____

_____

Name _____

extremely   weird   courageous   adventurous

Use the context clues in each sentence to help you decide which vocabulary word fits best in the blank.

Helga's Aunt Gerta invited her to go hiking. Aunt Gerta hiked all the time in the canyon near her house. She even took pictures as she hiked the trails. Helga always enjoyed looking at the photographs of trees, birds, and even _____ looking bugs that she had never seen before.

Helga was very excited about going hiking in the canyon. The last time she had done something _____ was a nature walk she took in the field behind her house. But that was hardly as daring and exciting as a hike in a canyon. Helga remembered one of her favorite stories about a _____ explorer who had been brave enough to climb Mount Everest. The canyon wasn't exactly Mount Everest, but it was a start.

There was a knock on the door. Helga ran to answer it, with her mother close behind. It was her aunt. "Are you ready for our adventure, Helga?" asked Aunt Gerta.

"More than you know!" said Helga. "Let me grab my backpack!"

"Your backpack is on the couch," said Helga's mother. "The summer sun is already shining brightly so it will be _____ hot on the trails. I put two bottles of cold water and some apple slices in there for you."

"Thanks, Mom!" said Helga. Then she ran to join Aunt Gerta for their hiking adventure.

Name _____

Read the selection. Complete the theme graphic organizer.

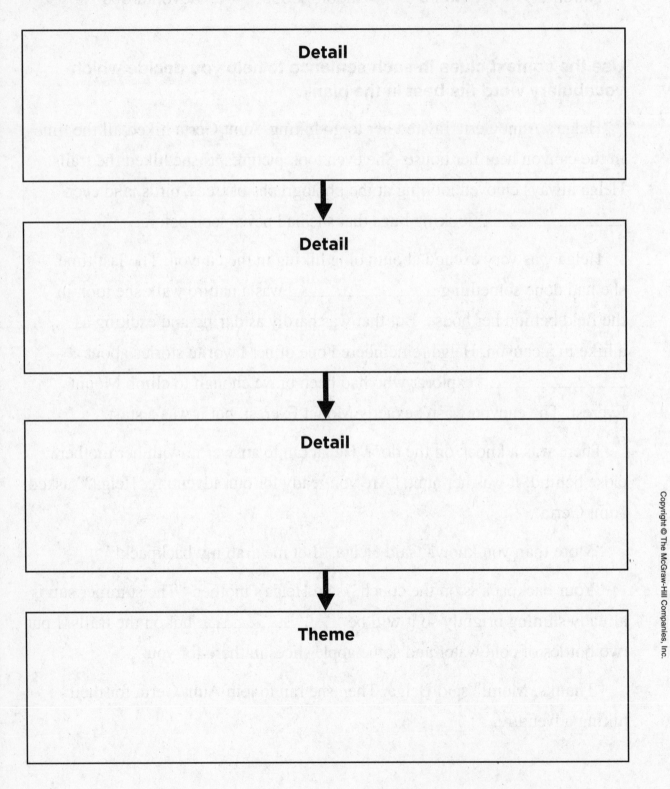

Detail

↓

Detail

↓

Detail

↓

Theme

Name _____

Read the poem. Check your understanding by asking yourself what message the author wants to share.

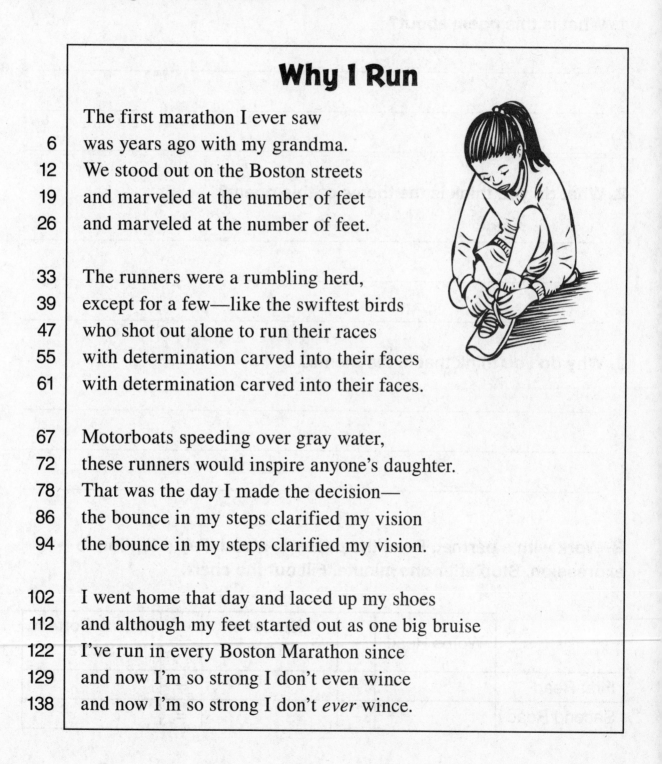

Why I Run

	The first marathon I ever saw
6	was years ago with my grandma.
12	We stood out on the Boston streets
19	and marveled at the number of feet
26	and marveled at the number of feet.
33	The runners were a rumbling herd,
39	except for a few—like the swiftest birds
47	who shot out alone to run their races
55	with determination carved into their faces
61	with determination carved into their faces.
67	Motorboats speeding over gray water,
72	these runners would inspire anyone's daughter.
78	That was the day I made the decision—
86	the bounce in my steps clarified my vision
94	the bounce in my steps clarified my vision.
102	I went home that day and laced up my shoes
112	and although my feet started out as one big bruise
122	I've run in every Boston Marathon since
129	and now I'm so strong I don't even wince
138	and now I'm so strong I don't *ever* wince.

Name _____

A. Reread the passage and answer the questions.

1. What is this poem about?

_____

_____

_____

2. What do you think is the theme of this poem?

_____

_____

_____

3. Why do you think that is the theme?

_____

_____

_____

B. Work with a partner. Read the passage aloud. Pay attention to expression. Stop after one minute. Fill out the chart.

	Words Read	–	Number of Errors	=	Words Correct Score
First Read		–		=	
Second Read		–		=	

Name _____

If I Could Just Get Out of Bed

If I get out of bed, I could
    read a book about the moon
      and one about a rocket ship
        and one that tells me how to make
          a ship that flies me into space
            to be the first kid on the moon
              if I get out of bed.

Answer the questions about the poem.

1. What makes this poem free verse?

_____

_____

2. Whose point of view is the poem written from?

_____

_____

3. What event is the speaker in the poem describing?

_____

_____

Name _____

Read the lines of the narrative poem below. Then follow the directions.

Why I Run

Motorboats speeding over gray water,
these runners would inspire anyone's daughter.
That was the day I made the decision—
the bounce in my steps clarified my vision
the bounce in my steps clarified my vision.

I went home that day and laced up my shoes
and although my feet started out as one big bruise
I've run in every Boston Marathon since
and now I'm so strong I don't even wince
and now I'm so strong I don't even wince.

---

1. **Find two examples of rhyme in the poem. Draw boxes around the words.**

2. **Circle an example of repetition in the poem.**

3. **Write another stanza for this poem that includes repetition and rhyme.**

   _____

   _____

   _____

   _____

   _____

Name _____

**Read each passage. Find the metaphor and write it on the line.
Then write the two things that are being compared.**

1. The runners were a rumbling herd,
   except for a few—

   _____

   _____

2. Motorboats speeding over gray water,
   these runners would inspire anyone's daughter.

   _____

   _____

3. I went home that day and laced up my shoes
   and although my feet started out as one big bruise

   _____

   _____

Name _____

A. Read each sentence. Underline the word with the soft c or soft g sound.

1. I learned to ice skate last winter.

2. We saw giant trees in the redwood forest.

3. Mom bought celery for the salad.

4. It was fun to sing on stage last night.

5. He drew a perfect circle on his paper.

B. Read each sentence. Write the correct form of the word shown below each line. Use -er or -est to complete the sentence.

1. Oak Park is _____ than Blue Lake Park.
   big

2. Mr. Landon's house is the _____ house in our entire town.
   old

3. January is always our _____ month.
   cold

4. Who is _____, you or your sister?
   young

5. I think this apple is _____ than the one I ate yesterday.
   sweet

Name _____

Evidence is details and examples from a text that support a writer's opinion. This student wrote an opinion about whether or not the author gives enough details in a poem to help figure out the theme.

Topic sentence →   In "Why I Run," the author shares details about running that help me figure out that people can be inspired to try new things. At the beginning of the

Evidence → poem, the narrator is watching a marathon. She feels inspired. I read that she thought the runners were like the swiftest birds, and they would inspire anyone's daughter. The narrator makes a decision to run. She has been running in every Boston

Concluding statement → Marathon since. The author's details help me figure out that the theme of the poem is that we can all be inspired to try new things by other people.

Write your opinion about a poem you read. Find text evidence to support your opinion of how the author gives enough details to help you figure out the main message or theme.

Write a topic sentence: _____

_____

Cite evidence from the text: _____

_____

_____

_____

End with a concluding statement: _____

_____

Name _____

A. Read the draft model. Use the questions that follow the draft to help you think about what strong words you can add.

Draft Model

Aunt Barb works really hard
She speaks three languages
Aunt Barb helps me fly
And never lets me fall

---

1. What strong words would tell how Aunt Barb works?

2. What languages does Aunt Barb speak?

3. What strong verbs or details would show how Aunt Barb helps the speaker fly?

B. Now revise the draft by adding strong words to make the poem clearer and more descriptive.

_____

_____

_____

_____

_____

_____

Name _____

admit	considered	humble	payment
creation	magnificent	reluctantly	barter

Use a word from the box to answer each question. Then use the word in a sentence.

1. **What did you do if you thought hard about a problem?** _____

_____

2. **What word means a *thing that was made*?** _____

_____

3. **What word could describe an amazing display of fireworks?**

_____

4. **What do people do when they make a trade?** _____

_____

5. **What is another word for *confess*?** _____

_____

6. **What word could describe something that is small and simple?**

_____

7. **What is another word for *unwillingly*?** _____

_____

8. **What word could describe the money you give for a purchase?**

_____

Name _____

Read the selection. Complete the point of view graphic organizer.

Details

↓

Point of View

Name _____

Read the passage. Use the summarize strategy to make sure you understand what you read.

Otomo Otomo Spins Gold

It is not easy to be a Japanese gnome. Nothing in the world
13 | is made to fit my size. That's one problem. Another problem is
25 | that everyone thinks that I am bad. Sometimes I play tricks on
37 | people. But that is rarely the case. I'll tell you a story and then
51 | you can decide for yourself.

56 | I was out for a walk, taking in the **scenery**, and I heard the
70 | **unmistakable** sound of a young woman crying. So I climbed the
81 | wall, brick by giant brick, up to the window. She told me that
94 | she had a big problem. She needed to turn a bale of hay into a
109 | string made of gold, using a spinning wheel—not just once, but
121 | every night for five nights. If she couldn't, a rich king would make
134 | her leave the kingdom.

138 | It just so happens that spinning straw into gold is my **specialty**.
150 | It is one of the perks of being a magical being. We all get
164 | something we are very good at. This is mine. So we made a deal.
178 | I would spin gold for her. All she had to do was guess my name.
193 | (It is Otomo Otomo.) She got three tries each of the five nights.
206 | If she couldn't guess it, then she'd come to live with me and my
220 | sisters. It seemed like a good deal to me. She seemed confident,
232 | so I shook her hand. Then I took the straw back to my house.

Name _____

The next night, I brought her gold, and she was **overjoyed**. She made terrible guesses about my name: Norman, Takemura, and Pete. I thought it would be very nice to have someone tall around to help clean the top of my bookshelf. I thought she would be very **comfortable** among my sisters and me in the forest.

So the next three nights happened in much the same way. I took her straw home, sat and sang my spinning songs, made her gold, and brought it back. Every night she made **uninformed**, wild guesses at my name. They were hard to listen to, since they were so bad. Really? She thought my name was Sylvester? No parent would name a son Sylvester.

So on the fifth and final night, I returned with the gold. She looked less defeated. She almost looked **relieved**. I started to get nervous, but I didn't want her to see that. I put the gold down, and asked, "What is my name?" She made her first two guesses: Roy and Yoshida. My tiny heart leaped at the promise of her company. But then she smiled and said, "Otomo Otomo. That is your name."

When I asked her how she knew my name, she told me that she heard me singing my songs the night before. My spinning songs all include my name. So I went home alone. You see? I am not cruel or mean. It was just a deal we made that ended badly for me. And there will always be someone who needs my help. Maybe you do. How about it? What do you need?

Name _____

A. Reread the passage and answer the questions.

1. What is Otomo Otomo's point of view about himself in the first paragraph?

_____

_____

_____

2. What is Otomo Otomo's point of view about his deal in paragraph 3?

_____

_____

_____

3. What is Otomo Otomo's point of view at the end of the passage?

_____

_____

_____

_____

B. Work with a partner. Read the passage aloud. Pay attention to intonation. Stop after one minute. Fill out the chart.

	Words Read	–	Number of Errors	=	Words Correct Score
First Read		–		=	
Second Read		–		=	

Name _____

The Dragon in the Apple Orchard

Once upon a time, an old man lived near an apple orchard. So much fruit grew in the orchard that the old man was able to get all the food he needed from it. In fact, years of getting his food so easily had made him lazy. It was fall and the apples were ripe, but the old man didn't feel like doing the work. "Why should I pick them now?" he thought. "They'll be there when I need them."

But one day the old man awoke to a terrible sight. A dragon had settled down right in the middle of the orchard and was eating the apples! The old man was afraid. "If that dragon eats all of my apples, what will I have to eat?" he thought as he looked on.

After a little while, the dragon fell asleep. The old man thought, "This is my chance!" He crept out to the orchard, picked all the apples he needed, and hurried home. "I will pick these sooner next year," he thought. "I'm not the only one who wants them!"

Answer the questions about the text.

1. How do you know that this text is a fairy tale?

_____

_____

2. What in the story couldn't happen in real life?

_____

_____

3. What literary element does this fairy tale have at the end?

_____

_____

4. What do you think the message or lesson of this fairy tale is?

_____

Name _____

Read each sentence below. Write the root word of the underlined word. Then write a definition of the underlined word.

1. We rode the train from Texas to Utah so that we could see trees, mountains, rivers and all other parts of the beautiful <u>scenery</u>.

_____

2. After I took a sip of the smoothie, the flavor of blueberry was <u>unmistakable</u>. I would know it anywhere!

_____

3. The performer can do many things but her <u>specialty</u> is singing.

_____

4. We were <u>overjoyed</u> and smiling ear to ear when our parents said we could adopt a puppy.

_____

5. I thought that my new shoes would hurt my feet, but instead they were quite <u>comfortable</u>.

_____

6. The <u>uninformed</u> guests did not know where they were supposed to sit.

_____

7. She was <u>relieved</u> to know that she earned an A even though her last project received a B-.

_____

Name _____

A. Make a compound word by adding a word part from the word box to the underlined word in each sentence. Write the word parts and compound word on the lines.

paper	walks	basket	day	bare

1. It's fun to take off our shoes and go <u>foot</u> at the beach.

   _____ + _____ = _____

2. Where can I buy today's <u>news</u>?

   _____ + _____ = _____

3. His dad will be the new <u>ball</u> coach.

   _____ + _____ = _____

4. I earn extra money by shoveling snow from the <u>side</u>.

   _____ + _____ = _____

5. Let's find the lost dog while we still have plenty of <u>light</u>.

   _____ + _____ = _____

B. Circle the word in each pair that has a consonant + *le, el, al, or il* final syllable. Write the word with a slash to divide the syllables.

1. **pencil**   **weekly**   _____

2. **bowl**   **final**   _____

3. **bugle**   **glass**   _____

4. **angel**   **lately**   _____

Name _____

Evidence is details and examples from a text that support a writer's ideas. The student who wrote the paragraph below found evidence to show how details support a character's point of view.

Topic sentence →   In "Otomo Otomo Spins Gold," the author gives many details about what Otomo Otomo thinks about the deal he makes with a woman. At the beginning

Evidence → of the story, Otomo Otomo agrees to spin gold for a woman. They make a deal. Otomo Otomo thinks it is a good deal. But, when the deal doesn't work out for him, Otomo Otomo is not sad. I read that he knows there will always be someone who needs his help.

Concluding statement → The author gives details about what Otomo Otomo thinks, and I figured out that he likes helping people. I agree because when things don't work out once, it doesn't mean they won't work out all the time.

Write a paragraph about a story you have read. Find text evidence to support your opinion of whether or not the author gives enough details to help you figure out a character's point of view.

Write a topic sentence: _____

_____

Cite evidence from the text: _____

_____

End with a concluding statement: _____

_____

Name _____

A. Read the draft model. Use the questions that follow the draft to help you think about how you can vary sentence structures.

Draft Model

I went to my friend Alex's house last Saturday. Alex had a blue marble that I liked. I had a red marble that Alex liked. We traded the marbles.

---

1. How could you make the first sentence more interesting by starting it in a different way?

2. How could you combine the second and third sentences to make a compound sentence?

3. How could you make the last sentence more interesting by starting it in a different way?

B. Now revise the draft by using different kinds of sentences to make this story about trading something with a friend more detailed and interesting.

_____

_____

_____

_____

_____

_____

Name _____

| frustration | gazed | recycling | remaining |
| tinkered | conservation | discouraged | jubilant |

Finish each sentence using the vocabulary word provided.

1. (recycling) We had a special class today _____

_____.

2. (tinkered) I watched my father _____

_____.

3. (gazed) He could see the brightly colored fireworks _____

_____.

4. (remaining) After she grabs a handful of grapes, _____

_____.

5. (conservation) Shutting off lights that are not in use _____

_____.

6. (frustration) When the little girl couldn't find her toy, _____

_____.

7. (jubilant) Every year at his birthday party, _____

_____.

8. (discouraged) I studied for the test _____

_____.

Name _____

Read the selection. Complete the point of view graphic organizer.

Details

↓

Point of View

Name _____

Read the passage. Use the summarize strategy to check your understanding as you read.

The Jar Garden

12	Jesse had been living in the city with her family for nearly three weeks. She had started school but so far she had only met
25	Hank, the boy from next door. Every day they walked to and
37	from school right past an old neglected playground. One Friday
47	on their way home they stopped and gazed in. Jesse was from
59	the country and could not bear to see the playground in this
71	condition.
72	"Look at this run-down place," she said, discouraged. "There's
81	litter all over. We can't even play here."
89	"We tried to clean it up a few years ago," Hank said. "We even
103	tried to create a garden. After a few weeks though, it was filled
116	with garbage again so we had no choice but to desert it."
128	Hank led Jesse to a small corner of the playground where
139	trampled plants lay on the ground. A few old garden tools and a
152	watering can were there. Hank could see a tear in Jesse's eye.
164	"I really miss my home in the country," she said. "There are so
177	many open fields and space to run and play."
186	Hank felt bad for Jesse and did not like the playground as
198	it was either. They agreed to meet back there early the next
210	morning.
211	Hank was already at the playground when Jesse showed up the
222	next day. He had carefully gathered several jars into a pile.
233	"Hi Hank," Jesse said. "Are you cleaning the playground?"

Name _____

"Yes, people threw out all of these jars," he said. "We should use them to start a new garden."

Jesse agreed and they went to work picking up trash and collecting the remaining jars. They peeled the labels and cleaned out the jars. As the day went on, some of Hank's friends walked by and saw what they were doing. Hank introduced them to Jesse.

"Nice to meet you," Jesse said shyly, and continued working.

"I'm Katie," one of Hank's friends said. "We see that you're trying to fix up the old garden. Can we help?"

Jesse could see that the playground and garden were important to them too. They all pitched in to clean the playground. Then they worked in the garden. They filled the clean jars with soil. Then they inserted seeds that Jesse got from her mother. They lined up the jars in a row and watered them.

"Let's meet here every day," Hank said proudly. "We'll guarantee it stays clean this time." They all agreed and went home.

Jesse's new friends made her feel welcome, and she wanted to do something nice to thank them for all of their hard work.

The next Monday they all walked to school together. As they passed the playground, they noticed that Jesse had rearranged the jars to spell out the word *Welcome*.

"What a great way to enter the playground!" Hank said.

They were all very thankful for their new place to spend time.

Name _____

A. Reread the passage and answer the questions.

1. What is Jesse's point of view about the playground and its condition in paragraph 2?

_____

_____

_____

2. What is Hank's point of view about Jesse and the playground in paragraphs 6 and 7?

_____

_____

_____

3. How do Hank and Jesse feel about cleaning up the playground and making it a garden at the end of the passage?

_____

_____

_____

B. Work with a partner. Read the passage aloud. Pay attention to phrasing. Stop after one minute. Fill out the chart.

	Words Read	–	Number of Errors	=	Words Correct Score
First Read		–		=	
Second Read		–		=	

Name _____

Musical Recycling

The Earth Day Science Fair was only a few days away, but Ted still didn't have any ideas. The good ones, like tree-planting and bottle and can drives, had been taken already. Ted angrily kicked at an empty plastic jug. It hit the side of the school with a deep thud.

Suddenly, Ted had an idea. He found a smaller plastic bottle and tapped it. It made a higher sound. Ted laughed as he ran off to start work on his plastic drum set.

Answer the questions about the text.

1. How can you tell that this story is realistic fiction?

_____

_____

2. What text feature does the story have?

_____

_____

3. How does the text feature show that the story is realistic?

_____

_____

Name _____

Read each sentence below. Underline the context clues that help you understand the meaning of each homograph in bold. Then write the definition of the homograph on the line.

1. Jesse was from the country and could not **bear** to see the playground in this condition.

    _____

2. After a few weeks though, the playground was filled with garbage again so we had no choice but to **desert** it.

    _____

3. A few old garden tools and a watering **can** were there.

    _____

4. As the day went on, some of Hank's friends walked by and **saw** what they were doing.

    _____

5. They lined up the jars in a **row** and put water in them.

    _____

Name _____

A. Add the ending -s, -ed, or -ing to each word. Write the new word on the line.

1. name + ing = _____

2. hope + ed = _____

3. dance + s = _____

4. drop + ing = _____

5. wrap + ed = _____

B. Match a word in the box to each correct meaning below. Write the word on the line. Not all words will be used.

helpful	usable	useful	meaningful
painful	colorless	cheerful	colorful
meaningless	careful	painless	useless

1. full of cheer _____

2. can be used _____

3. without meaning _____

4. full of color _____

5. without pain _____

Name _____

Evidence is details and examples from a text that support a writer's opinion. The student who wrote the paragraph below wrote an opinion about whether or not the author gives enough details to figure out Hank's point of view.

Topic sentence →   In "The Jar Garden," the author gives many details that support Hank's point of view. At the beginning of the story, Hank sees how the run-down playground makes Jesse miss where she used to live. I read that Hank wants to clean up the playground. So Hank, Jesse, and some friends work together to clean the playground. At the end of the story, Hank is proud that they have a new place to play. The author gives many details that help me figure out that Hank thinks a clean playground will make Jesse feel happy. I agree with Hank because Jesse was sad about the dirty playground.

Evidence →

Concluding statement →

Write about a story you have read. Find text evidence to support your opinion about whether or not the author gives enough information to figure out the character's point of view. Do you agree? Explain.

Write a topic sentence: _____

_____

Cite evidence from the text: _____

_____

_____

End with a concluding statement: _____

_____

Name _____

A. Read the draft model. Use questions that follow the draft to help you think about what sensory language you can add.

Draft Model

  We went to a wedding this weekend. I did not have a suit to wear. My mom gave me my brother's old suit to wear. It did not fit, but I wore it anyway.

---

1. Where was the wedding? Whose wedding was it?

2. Why did the narrator not have a suit to wear?

3. What sensory details could you use to describe the brother's old suit?

4. What sensory details could be added to help readers picture the wedding?

B. Now revise the draft by using sensory language to describe the suit and the wedding.

_____

_____

_____

_____

_____

Name _____

| equipment | accidental | purpose | respond |
| disasters | prevention | harmful | careless |

Use a word from the box to answer each question. Then use the word in a sentence.

1. If something could possibly hurt you, what would you call it?

_____

2. What is the name of the tools needed to complete a job?

_____

3. What is another word for *the reason something is done*?

_____

4. What word might describe someone who is not paying attention?

_____

5. When something happens for no apparent reason, what is it called?

_____

6. What is another word for *unfortunate events*?

_____

7. What word might be used to say *stopping*?

_____

Name _____

Read the selection. Complete the author's point of view graphic organizer.

Details

↓

Author's Point of View

Name _____

Read the passage. Use the ask and answer questions strategy to check your understanding of important details in the passage.

True Teamwork

	We try to predict, or know, about emergencies before they
10	happen. They can come as a surprise though. Even if we can't
22	predict, we can prepare. In an emergency, it is best for people
34	to work as a team. When people work together they are more
46	prepared. They can help more people than if they were alone
57	and unprepared.
59	On August 29, 2005, Hurricane Katrina struck Louisiana.
67	It was one of the strongest storms to hit that area in the last 100
82	years. The high winds, heavy rains, and extreme floods destroyed
92	homes, buildings, land, and roads on the Gulf Coast. Some
102	people lost all they had. They lost their homes, clothes, cars,
113	and more. These people needed help. Teams were formed to give
124	relief, or help, to them. These teams came together to give food
136	and shelter. This was a hard time for the victims, or people hurt
149	by the storm. To find food and shelter on their own would have
162	been hard.
164	We do not always know when a storm, flood, or other event
176	is coming. Even so, there are teams who are always ready to help.
189	When something like Katrina happens, they know what to do.
199	They know how to get food, water, and even doctors to people. It
212	is their job to work as a team and give help all over the world.

Name _____

Win Henderson/FEMA photo

It is good to know that there are teams who can help after a disaster. However, your family should still be prepared. It is important to know how to work as a team in an emergency. It can be as simple as talking to your neighbors. All of you can work together to be prepared.

Working as a team is encouraging and gives you hope. You all have the same goal. It might be a lot of work to prepare for an emergency alone. If you know your neighbors are working with you, it can make you feel better. You can all work together to be prepared. What should you do? One important thing is that everyone has a "Go Kit." This is a kit that has essential or important things you need to survive. It can have food, water, and flashlights in it. What if you forget to pack a flashlight? You might need one in an emergency. If your neighbors have packed one, they can help you. This is just one small benefit from working as a team.

Nobody knows for sure when an emergency might happen. It could be today or years from now. Perhaps you might never need to use your Go Kit. Yet knowing that you and your neighbors are ready and can work as a team makes everyone feel better. People feel more secure working as a team in an emergency than working alone.

Name _____

A. Reread the passage and answer the questions.

1. What does the first paragraph tell you about how the author feels about working as a team?

_____

_____

_____

2. How do you think the author would have felt about the teams who helped victims of Katrina?

_____

_____

_____

3. How do your opinions and feelings about working as a team compare with the author's?

_____

_____

_____

B. Work with a partner. Read the passage aloud. Pay attention to phrasing and rate. Stop after one minute. Fill out the chart.

	Words Read	–	Number of Errors	=	Words Correct Score
First Read		–		=	
Second Read		–		=	

Name _____

Teamwork at the Airport

When a plane is about to land, the pilot radios the air traffic controller to say that the plane is approaching. Then the air traffic controller looks at the runway to make sure that it is clear. If there are no planes on it, the controller tells the pilot to land.

Once the plane is on the ground the air traffic controller connects the pilot to a ground traffic controller. The ground traffic controller gives the plane a clear route from runway to airport.

The air traffic controller helps the pilot land.

The ground traffic controller guides the pilot to the airport.

Answer the questions about the text.

1. What genre is this? How can you tell?

_____

_____

2. Name the text feature. What purpose does it serve?

_____

_____

3. How do the pilot and the controllers work together to land a plane?

_____

_____

Name _____

Read the sentences. Underline the sentence clues that help you understand the meaning of each word in bold. Write the meaning of each word on the line.

1. When the pop quiz was announced Rita suddenly wished she had been able to **predict** it ahead of time.

   Predict means _____

2. Having a teacher tell her that she was a great student was **encouraging** to Gretel and gave her more confidence to do even better in class.

   Encouraging means _____

3. The sinking of the *Titanic* was a **tragedy**, or an unfortunate event, that people still talk about to this day.

   Tragedy means _____

4. After the earthquake, the Red Cross provided **relief**. The much needed support and help was amazing.

   Relief means _____

5. It was hard to tell at first how many **victims**, or people suffering from the destruction, of the flood there were.

   Victims means _____

6. If you are hiking, it is **essential** to have a map. It is also absolutely necessary to bring food and water with you.

   Essential means _____

Name _____

A. When a syllable ends in a consonant, it is called a closed syllable. Circle the words that have two closed syllables. Then write the syllables on the lines.

1. basket   refill   _____   _____

2. lesson   robot   _____   _____

3. tiny   problem   _____   _____

4. diner   napkin   _____   _____

5. rabbit   army   _____   _____

6. tiger   number   _____   _____

B. Related words have a common root or base word. Read each set of words. Circle the related words.

1. pedal   scouting   pedestrian

2. geology   geography   graceful

3. matter   magnify   magnificent

4. bicycle   tricycle   automobile

5. remain   renumber   numeral

Name _____

Evidence is details and examples from a text that support a writer's ideas. The student who wrote the paragraph below found evidence to show how details support the author's point of view.

Topic sentence →   In "True Teamwork," the author thinks being prepared and working together during emergencies is important. The author explains that in an emergency,

Evidence → it is best for people to work as a team. I also read that working together as a team is encouraging and gives people hope. The text also states that everyone feels better knowing that they are ready and can work together as a team in emergencies. There are many

Concluding statement → details that show that the author thinks working together and being prepared are good things during emergencies. I agree with the author's point of view because being ready and working as a team makes me feel safer and ready in an emergency.

Write a paragraph about a text you have read. Find text evidence to show details that support the author's point of view. Then explain whether or not you agree with the author's point of view and why.

Write a topic sentence: _____

_____

Cite evidence from the text: _____

_____

_____

End with a concluding statement: _____

_____

Name _____

A. Read the draft model. Use questions that follow the draft to help you create a strong paragraph.

Draft Model

One of a police officer's duties is to stop crime. They have radios to tell them where a crime is happening. Police officers arrest criminals so they can't commit any more crimes.

---

1. What is the main idea of the draft model? What topic sentence could you add to show this?

2. Do all of the other sentences support the main idea? Should any be deleted?

3. How can you strengthen the connection between the supporting sentences and the main idea?

4. Why are police officers important to a community?

B. Now revise the draft by creating a strong paragraph with a topic sentence and supporting sentences about police officers.

_____

_____

_____

_____

Name _____

citizenship	daring	participate	unfairness
continued	horrified	proposed	waver

Use the context clues in each sentence to help you decide which vocabulary word fits best in the blank.

Jeremy was in Mr. Hale's third grade class. This week they were learning about the rights of citizens. Mr. Hale told the class that voting was a big part of _____.

"In the past there were unjust rules that stopped some people from voting," said Mr. Hale. Jeremy was shocked. He was _____ by the _____ of these rules.

"How did they get the right to vote?" asked Jeremy.

"It was difficult," said Mr. Hale. "They had to be brave and sometimes _____. When others tried to stop them, they did not pause or _____. They _____ to fight for their rights. They wanted to _____ in the voting process."

Mr. Hale's words got Jeremy thinking. Later in the day, he _____ that the class write a play about people fighting for their right to vote.

"That's a great suggestion, Jeremy!" said Mr. Hale.

Name _____

Read the selection. Complete the author's point of view graphic organizer.

Details

Author's Point of View

Name _____

Read the passage. Use the ask and answer questions strategy to help you understand the text.

Hiram Revels – The First African American Senator

	Hiram Rhodes Revels was born in North Carolina in the year
11	1827. Through his whole life he was a good citizen. He was a
24	great teacher and leader. And he was always fair. He was so well
37	respected that he became the first African American to serve in
48	the U.S. Senate.
51	**A Hard Time for African Americans**
57	Revels was born during a hard time for African Americans.
67	African Americans were treated badly. Most African Americans
75	in the South were enslaved. Revels grew up as a free African
87	American, or freedman, however. As a freedman, Revels could
96	make his own choices.
100	Still, the laws in the South were unfair toward all African
111	Americans. They had to work hard jobs. They were not allowed
122	to go to school. Though it was not legal, some freedmen ran
134	schools for African American children. As a child, Revels was
144	sent to one of these schools. He worked hard to become highly
156	educated. He was unable to go to college in the South. So he
169	traveled far from home. He went to college in northern states.

Name _____

Preaching and Teaching

After college, Revels became the pastor of a church. He was a great speaker. He was also a great teacher. Revels knew many people did not want African Americans to be educated. But Revels was very brave. He traveled all over the country. He taught African Americans. He knew that this would make them good citizens.

The First African American Senator

Revels moved to Natchez, Mississippi, in 1866. By this time, slavery had been banned. There were many newly freed African Americans. These freedmen voted for Revels to be in the Mississippi State Senate. From there, he was elected to the U.S. Senate. He was the first African American to become a U.S. senator. It was a great achievement!

In the Senate, Revels tried to be fair to all the people in his state. He disliked rules that were unfair for African Americans. So he tried to change them. He made it legal for African Americans to work in the Navy's shipyards. He challenged rules that kept African Americans apart from other Americans. But he was also fair to people of all colors. Even though the South lost during the Civil War, Revels did not want white southern soldiers to be punished.

Hiram Revels helped many people throughout his life. He helped people learn. As a senator, he helped the country progress. He was truly a good citizen!

Hiram Rhodes Revels: the first African American to serve in the U.S. Senate.

Name _____

A. Reread the passage and answer the questions.

1. How does the author describe Revels in paragraph 1?

_____

_____

2. What did Revels do that the author describes as "brave"?

_____

_____

3. According to the text, what was Revels's "great achievement"?

_____

_____

4. What is the author's position about Hiram Revels?

_____

_____

B. Work with a partner. Read the passage aloud. Pay attention to phrasing and rate. Stop after one minute. Fill out the chart.

	Words Read	–	Number of Errors	=	Words Correct Score
First Read		–		=	
Second Read		–		=	

Name _____

Jane Addams's Early Years

Jane Addams always knew that she wanted to help people. However, after she finished school in Illinois, she was not sure how best to plan her life's work. She attended medical school, but she did not finish. When she took a trip to Europe, Addams visited Toynbee Hall in London, England. Toynbee Hall had been founded to help poor and homeless people. It offered classes and activities. This community center gave her ideas for a center that she would later found in Chicago: Hull House.

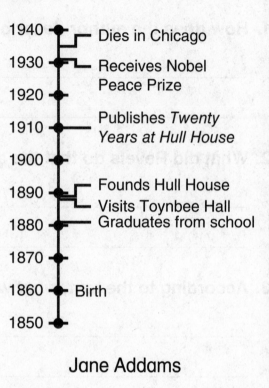

Jane Addams

Answer the questions about the text.

1. How do you know that this text is a biography?

_____

2. What text feature does this biography include? _____

3. How does the text feature help you understand Addams's life better?

_____

4. Where did Jane Addams get her ideas for founding Hull House?

_____

Name _____

Read each sentence below. Underline the word in each sentence that has the prefix *un-* or *dis-* or the suffix *-ly*. Then write the meaning of the word on the line.

1. African Americans were treated badly.

_____

2. Still, the laws in the South were unfair toward all African Americans.

_____

3. He worked hard to become highly educated.

_____

4. He was unable to go to college in the South.

_____

5. There were many newly freed African Americans.

_____

6. He disliked rules that were not fair for African Americans.

_____

Name _____

A. Add the endings to each word. Write the new word on the line. Pay attention to possible spelling changes.

1. try + ing   =   _____

2. dry + ed   =   _____

3. hurry + s   =   _____

4. play + ing   =   _____

5. study + ed   =   _____

B. Match a word in the box to each meaning below. Write the word on the line. Not all words will be used.

liveliness	respectful	delightful	respectless
colorless	happiness	colorful	soundless

1. without color   _____

2. state of being happy   _____

3. full of delight   _____

4. without sound   _____

5. state of being lively   _____

6. full of respect   _____

Name _____

Evidence is details and examples from a text that support a writer's opinion. This student wrote about whether or not the author's use of text features helps him understand more about Hiram Rhodes Revels.

Topic sentence → In "Hiram Revels – The First African American Senator," the author uses headings to help organize information and an illustration to help me understand more about Hiram Revels. In the first

Evidence → section, "A Hard Time for African Americans," the author tells about what life was like for Hiram as a young student. In the section "Preaching and Teaching," the author describes what Revels did after college. There is also an illustration, which shows what Hiram looked like. The caption gives me more information about Hiram. The author's use

Concluding statement → of headings helps me better understand the events in Hiram's life, and the illustration helps me picture what he looked like.

Write a paragraph about a text you read. Find text evidence to support your opinion about the author's use of text features.

Write a topic sentence: _____

_____

Cite evidence from the text: _____

_____

_____

End with a concluding statement: _____

_____

Name _____

A. Read the draft model. Use the questions that follow the draft to help you think about how you can grab the reader's attention with a strong opening.

Draft Model

My grandmother is a good citizen because it improves our community. She volunteers at the park so kids have a safe place to play. My Uncle is a good citizen because it keeps us safe. He volunteers as a firefighter to protect people and property.

---

1. What is the purpose of this text?

2. What opening sentence would clearly state the topic and grab the reader's attention?

3. What opening would make readers want to read more?

B. Now revise the draft by adding a strong opening to make readers want to read more.

_____

_____

_____

_____

_____

_____

Name _____

produce	replace	energy	natural
sources	traditional	renewable	pollution

Finish each sentence using the vocabulary word provided.

1. **(traditional)** We are going over to our friend's house _____

   _____ .

2. **(sources)** The sun and the wind _____

   _____ .

3. **(produce)** Our science teacher asked us _____

   _____ .

4. **(energy)** I slept for eight hours _____

   _____ .

5. **(replace)** Our old television broke, _____

   _____ .

6. **(pollution)** We bought an electric car _____

   _____ .

7. **(natural)** This store only sells _____

   _____ .

8. **(renewable)** The tomatoes in our garden _____

   _____ .

Name _____

Read the selection. Complete the cause and effect graphic organizer.

Cause	➡	Effect
First ➡		
Next ➡		
Then ➡		
Finally ➡		

Name _____

Read the passage. Use the ask and answer questions strategy to find answers to your questions in the passage.

The Electric Car

Have you ever seen a person plug in a car? Some cars use
13   electricity to run instead of gasoline. There are many good
23   reasons to buy an electric-powered car. But there are also some
34   downsides to keep in mind.

39   **Electric Car History**

42   An electric car runs on an electric motor. The car uses a foot
55   pedal to move just like any other car. But it uses a battery to
69   power the motor, not gas. Common household electricity is used
79   to recharge the electric car battery.

85   Electric engines got their start in the 1830s. For years they
96   were improved. Better batteries were made. By the late 1800s the
107 cars were used by many people in the United States.

117 The electric cars were easy to drive. Drivers did not have to
129 change gears. Gas-powered cars needed a hand crank to get
139 started. Electric cars did not.

144 Many people used electric cars in cities. The cars drove
154 smoothly. They made little noise. They also didn't have the
164 smell of gas cars. Electric cars were even used as New York
176 taxis in 1897.

179 Then Henry Ford made the gas-powered Model T in 1908. It
190 ran better than the old gas cars. It was cheaper to produce than
203 electric cars. It ended the reign of the electric car.

Name _____

Pros and Cons

There are many reasons for people to buy electric cars today. They are good for the planet. They do not let pollution out into the air. Gas-powered cars use a tailpipe to let pollution escape.

Electric cars don't need the upkeep that gas cars need. No oil changes. No trips to the gas station. There are fewer parts to an electric engine. This often means fewer problems.

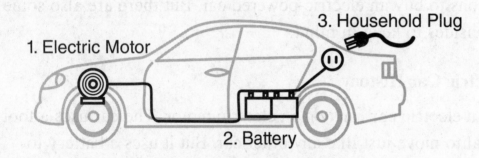

The Main Parts of the Electric Car

There are a few drawbacks to an electric-powered car though. One thing is that it has to be charged. Charging times can vary. A full charge can take up to a few hours.

Most electric cars can only go so far on one electric charge. A gasoline car can go farther on a full tank of gas. And there are plenty of gas stations around. Yet, there are not many places to recharge an electric car.

Electric car batteries may also need to be replaced. They cost a lot of money. They are also big and heavy.

The electric car has been around a long time. The future is bright if car makers keep working to make it better.

Name _____

A. Reread the passage and answer the questions.

1. What were some things that caused people to buy electric cars in the late 1800s?

   _____

   _____

   _____

2. What was the effect of the Model T?

   _____

   _____

   _____

3. What is a possible effect of the following cause? *An electric-powered car needs to be charged and there are not a lot of places to recharge it while on the road.* Use the information under the heading **Pros and Cons** to help you.

   _____

   _____

B. Work with a partner. Read the passage aloud. Pay attention to rate. Stop after one minute. Fill out the chart.

	Words Read	–	Number of Errors	=	Words Correct Score
First Read		–		=	
Second Read		–		=	

Name _____

Energy from Recycled Plastic

Some kinds of plastic can only be recycled a certain number of times. After that, these plastics cannot be used for anything and must be taken to a landfill. Luckily, scientists have recently performed experiments which prove that we can burn this useless plastic to create energy. The next step is to put this process into practice so that power plants around the country are able to use these plastics as fuel.

The Search for New Energy

Today, finding new sources of energy is of the highest importance. We can now add plastic to wind, sun, and water as an alternative source of energy. But even as we work to build power plants that burn recycled plastic as fuel, we must continue to look for new energy sources to replace dirty fossil fuels.

Answer the questions about the text.

1. **How can you tell that this is an informational text?**

   _____

2. **What text feature does it include?**

   _____

3. **What opinion does the author express in the text feature?**

   _____

   _____

Name _____

Read each sentence below. Underline the context clues that help you understand the meaning of each homophone in bold. Then write the correct definition of the homophone on the line.

1. Have you ever **seen** a person plug in a car?

_____

2. The car uses a foot **pedal** to move just like any other car.

_____

3. Electric engines got their start **in** the 1830s.

_____

4. The Model T ended the **reign** of the electric car.

_____

5. **One** thing that the electric car needs is to be charged.

_____

Name _____

A. Read the words in each row. Circle the word in the row that has one or more open syllables. Then write the circled word's syllables on the lines.

1. giant   silver   _____   _____

2. parking   paper   _____   _____

3. legal   flutter   _____   _____

4. pillow   notice   _____   _____

5. photo   curtain   _____   _____

6. pencil   polar   _____   _____

B. Read the words in the box below. Match each word to the correct meaning by writing the word on the line.

usable	remake	carefully
unwilling	cheerful	respectful

1. not willing   _____

2. to make again   _____

3. able to be used   _____

4. in a careful way   _____

5. full of cheer   _____

6. full of respect   _____

Name _____

Evidence is details and examples from a text that support a writer's ideas. The student who wrote the paragraph below found evidence to show how the author uses a diagram to give important details about a topic.

Topic sentence → In "The Electric Car," the author uses a diagram to give important details about the electric car. **Evidence** → In the section, "Pros and Cons," the author uses a diagram of an electric car to show that it has a battery, an electric motor, and uses a household plug. This gives me more information and helps me understand the author's explanation of how the electric car works. I can look at the diagram and understand more about it. **Concluding statement** → The author uses a diagram to give more important details that help me understand more about the electric car.

Write a paragraph about a text you have read that includes a diagram. Find text evidence to show how the author uses a diagram to give important details about a topic.

Write a topic sentence: _____

_____

Cite evidence from the text: _____

_____

_____

_____

End with a concluding statement: _____

_____

Name _____

A. Read the draft model. Use the questions that follow the draft to help you think about how you can use voice to show your thoughts about a topic.

Draft Model

Regular cars waste energy. Electric cars run on electricity. Regular cars pollute the air. Electric cars can be charged right on the street. I want to have an electric car when I'm old enough to drive.

1. What does the author probably believe about wasting energy?

2. Why does the author think we should care about pollution?

3. What important things does the author believe electric cars can help with?

4. What is the writer's viewpoint about electric cars?

B. Now revise the draft by adding beliefs and reasons to help the writer voice an opinion.

_____

_____

_____

_____

_____

_____

Name _____

possess	necessary	treasure	alarmed
obsessed	reward	anguish	wealth

Use the context clues in each sentence to help you decide which vocabulary word fits best in the blank.

"Guess what I just read?" said Mary. "It was an exciting story about two friends looking for a secret _____, something of great value hidden in a jungle. Finding it was all they could think about. They were _____!"

"Well, do they find it?" asked Charlene.

"I won't tell you the end. It's _____ for you to read the book to find out. I will tell you, though, that the two friends go on a great adventure. They want to _____ the valuable item to have it for their own. So they follow a map."

"That sounds exciting!" said Charlene.

"It is! But little do they know that someone else has seen their map, someone who wants all the _____ and money that the map promises."

"Oh, no!" said Charlene. She sounded _____, worried about what might happen in the story.

"The two friends soon find out that someone else is following their map. They think someone else might find the _____ at the end of the map before they do. But they want the prize for themselves!"

"Oh, my goodness," said Charlene. "After following the map and going on such an adventure, it must fill them with _____ to think that someone might find the prize before them. They must be so worried. What happens next?"

Mary handed the book to Charlene. "Like I said, you have to read it!"

Charlene raced home, eager to read about the adventure Mary described.

Name _____

Read the selection. Complete the theme graphic organizer.

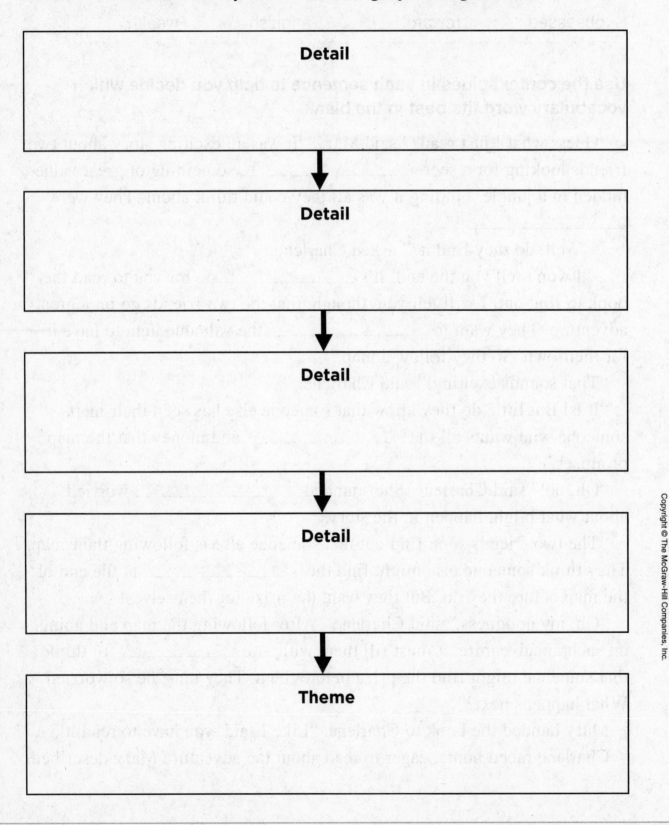

Detail

↓

Detail

↓

Detail

↓

Detail

↓

Theme

Name _____

Read the passage. Use the make predictions strategy to check your understanding as you read.

Prometheus Brings Fire to Humans

Cast:

1	Narrator | Prometheus | Zeus | Human 1 | Human 2
8	Scene 1
10	*Setting: Mount Olympus, the home of the ancient Greek gods.*
20	*Zeus sits on a throne in the middle of the stage. There is a*
34	*fireplace with a roaring fire in it to his left. Prometheus enters.*
46	**Zeus:** Prometheus! Welcome to my throne room! I trust
55	everything is good.
58	**Prometheus:** I'm afraid not, Lord Zeus. I have been to Earth
69	and lived among the people. They are miserable. They live in
80	caves and eat raw meat. When winter comes, they die of cold and
93	starvation. I would like to ask you to share fire with them.
105	I believe it would help them keep warm and cook their meat.
117	**Zeus:** Absolutely not! If humans have fire, they might become
127	strong and wise like the gods. They could force us from our
139	kingdom. I am happy to keep them cold and uninformed. That
150	way we gods can rule the world unthreatened and happy.
160	**Prometheus:** *(under his breath)* But I am not a god. I am a
173	Titan. If you will not help them, I will! *(he exits)*

Name _____

Scene 2

Narrator: (Voice over) Prometheus wanted to do something to help humans. One day, walking along the seashore, he found a reed sticking out of the water. It was soft and dry on the inside—perfect for carrying fire. So Prometheus traveled to the end of the earth, where the morning sun lives, and touched his reed to the fires that light the sun. Then he quickly returned to his homeland, so he could share the fire with the humans he knew.

Setting: Prometheus is standing outside of a cave with some humans dressed in animal furs.

Prometheus: Look! *(he touches his reed to a pile of sticks and a fire lights)* I have brought you the secret to your empowerment! This is the fire that will change your life!

Human 1: What do we do with it?

Prometheus: You can use it to cook meat or keep warm. It will let you leave your caves to experience the world. When you are warm and well fed, it is much easier to do anything you want!

Human 2: Why would you do this for us?

Prometheus: I know how hard it is to live someplace that doesn't seem to want you. It is important to me that, given the chance, I can help you become the creatures I know you must become. I only ask that you also help those less fortunate when you have the chance.

Narrator: The humans agreed to Prometheus's request. Then they began the slow process of bringing about a world in which they could live in happiness without suffering.

Name _____

A. Reread the passage and answer the questions.

1. How does Prometheus describe humans to Zeus?

_____

_____

2. What does Prometheus want to do to help humans?

_____

_____

3. List some ways Prometheus thinks fire will help improve the lives of humans.

_____

_____

4. What is the theme of this story?

_____

_____

B. Work with a partner. Read the passage aloud. Pay attention to expression. Stop after one minute. Fill out the chart.

	Words Read	–	Number of Errors	=	Words Correct Score
First Read		–		=	
Second Read		–		=	

Name _____

Scene 3: The Fall of Icarus

Daedalus and his son, Icarus, have escaped from the island of Crete where the king had held them captive. They are flying above the sea, using the wings Daedalus has built.

DAEDALUS: Stay close to me, Icarus. We have a long way to fly! Be safe.

ICARUS: But Father, when will I ever have another chance to see the sun so close?

DAEDALUS: If you fly too high, the sun will melt the wax holding your wings together!

ICARUS: Don't worry, I'll pay close attention. If the wax starts to melt, I'll come down.

DAEDALUS: If the wax starts to melt, it will be too late! Come down now!

ICARUS: But you should see the view from up here! I can see every island in the sea! What an incredible sight! *The wax in Icarus's wings begins to melt; his wings no longer work properly, and he struggles to stay in the air.*

DAEDALUS: *Shouting.* Icarus! Your wings!

Answer the questions about the text.

1. How do you know this text is a drama?

_____

_____

2. Do you think being safe is important to Icarus? Why or why not?

_____

_____

Name _____

Read each sentence below. Write the root word of the word in bold on the line. Then write the definition of the word in bold.

1. I have been to Earth and lived among the people. They are **miserable**.

_____

2. When winter comes, they die of cold and **starvation**.

_____

3. I am happy to keep them cold and **uninformed**.

_____

4. That way we gods can rule the world **unthreatened** and happy.

_____

5. I have brought you the secret to your **empowerment!**

_____

6. I only ask that you also help those less **fortunate** when you have the chance.

_____

Name _____

A. Read each sentence. Underline the word that has a prefix. Write the meaning of the word on the line.

1. My model ship fell off the table, and now I have to rebuild it.

   _____

2. Of all the vegetables on the table, I dislike peas the most.

   _____

3. Before my sister started kindergarten, she went to preschool.

   _____

4. When I fell into the mud puddle, I knew I was having an unlucky day.

   _____

5. I lost my copy of the story, so I need to reprint it before class.

   _____

B. Related words have a common root or base word. Read each set of words. Circle the words that have a common root or base word.

1. alike   unlike   click

2. precook   pretty   cooking

3. halfway   unhappy   happily

4. review   viewing   voting

5. unlucky   cluck   luckily

Name _____

Evidence is details and examples from a text that support a writer's ideas. The student who wrote the paragraph below found evidence to show how the author uses dialogue, setting, and stage directions to tell a story.

Topic sentence →   In "Prometheus Brings Fire to Humans," the author uses dialogue, scenes, and stage directions to tell a story. The dialogue, scenes, and stage directions

Evidence → tell me what is happening in the play. Each scene tells part of the story in time order. In Scene 1, Zeus and Prometheus are talking, and Prometheus says something under his breath. This stage direction tells me that he has a plan and does not want Zeus to hear it. From the dialogue, I can tell that they do not agree.

Concluding statement → The author uses dialogue, scenes, and stage directions to tell about the characters and the events in a play.

Write a paragraph about a play you have read. Find text evidence to show how the author uses dialogue, scenes, and stage directions to tell the story.

Write a topic sentence: _____

_____

Cite evidence from the text: _____

_____

_____

_____

End with a concluding statement: _____

_____

Name _____

A. Read the draft model. Use the questions that follow the draft to help you vary sentence lengths.

Draft Model

My apron is important to me. My mother wore it when she was a girl. I wear it now when I am spending time with my mother, just like she did.

---

1. How could the writer combine the first and second sentences?

2. What short fourth sentence could the writer add after the long third sentence to vary the rhythm?

3. Can any of the sentences be deleted?

4. How might you improve the rhythm of the writing? How might you vary sentence length?

B. Now revise the draft by creating sentence fluency with a combination of long and short sentences about something the writer values.

_____

_____

_____

_____

_____

Name _____

> | forecast | relief | forbidding | stranded |
> | argue | astonished | conditions | complained |

Finish each sentence using the vocabulary word provided.

1. **(stranded) When the bus wouldn't start,** _____

   _____.

2. **(conditions) During the winter months** _____

   _____.

3. **(argue) It is not polite** _____

   _____.

4. **(forbidding) There was a large sign** _____

   _____.

5. **(complained) After the terrible movie** _____

   _____.

6. **(relief) When the long race ended** _____

   _____.

7. **(astonished) My classmates** _____

   _____.

8. **(forecast) This week** _____

   _____.

Name _____

Read the selection. Complete the theme graphic organizer.

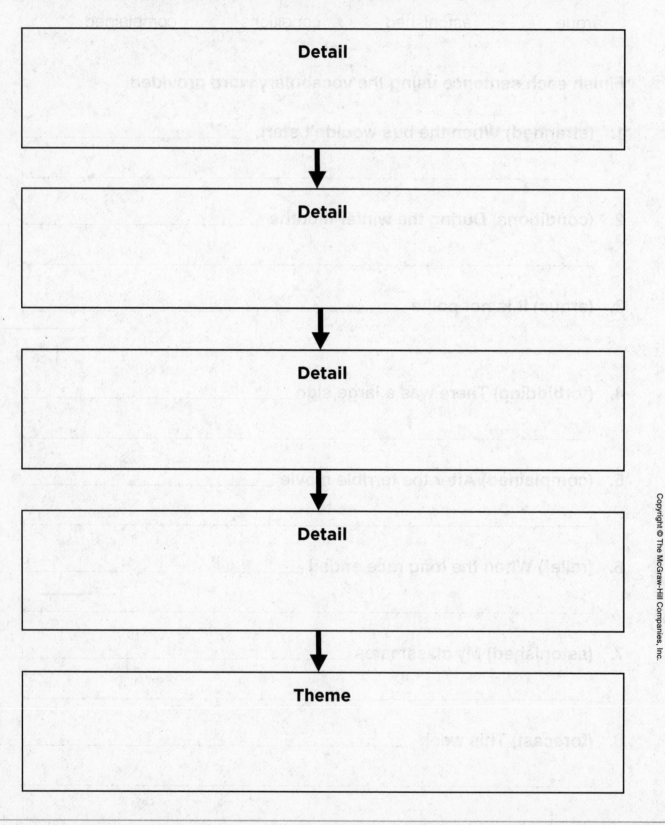

Detail

Detail

Detail

Detail

Theme

Name _____

**Read the passage. Use the make predictions strategy
to check your understanding as you read.**

Warm Enough for Wheat

	I live on a farm in the Middle Colonies. Living here is
12	what I have always known. I was the first of my family born
25	here. My parents and two sisters came here from England,
35	though. I often ask Father what life was like before I was born.
48	He's always so proud to tell me. My family was brave to leave
61	all they knew to start a new life here. Strangely enough, it was
74	the weather that helped my family decide where they would live
85	in this new land.
89	My father likes adventure. Mother says that if he isn't
99	exploring, Father is at sixes and sevens and he doesn't know
110	what to do with himself! So when my Uncle Charles moved to
122	New England, Father knew it was time for a change, too. Moving
134	to New England would mean adventure and a new life.
144	When my family came to New England, they lived with Uncle
155	Charles for a few months. Uncle Charles had become a fisherman
166	in New England. Since it was so cold in the winter, it was hard
180	to have a farm. Many people there were fishermen because it
191	was more reliable for them to fish than to grow food. They could
204	trade the fish for other food. Trying to grow crops in the rocky
217	soil that was covered in snow for months at a time was difficult.

Name _____

Father tried his hand at fishing, but he wasn't much of a success. He found that he didn't like being on the boat! He must not have had sea legs. The more he thought about it, the more he knew he wanted to be a farmer. He had heard people from the Middle Colonies speak of their farms. It sounded like the life he had dreamt of.

After sleeping on it and giving it a lot of thought, my parents bought a farm in the Middle Colonies. The Middle Colonies had a warmer climate than New England. Because of the milder weather, farming was less difficult. For the next three years, they grew grains on the farm. In fact, the Middle  Colonies are called the Bread Basket. That is because of all the grains grown here. Having a successful grain farm north in New England would not have been possible. Thanks to the warmer weather farther south, my family had found the life they wanted.

The farm did quite well. My mother even opened a bakery in town. Not long after that, I was born. I've been helping on the farm and in the bakery ever since I can remember. The weather sure had an effect on where my family decided to live. We couldn't have had the same life farther north. My family found adventure, a new home, and a family business. Our life is the best life I can think of—it takes the cake! I know my parents made the right choice.

Name _____

A. Reread the passage and answer the questions.

1. In paragraph 1, what does the narrator say helped the family decide where they would move?

_____

_____

_____

2. What are two reasons the family moved from New England to the Middle Colonies?

_____

_____

_____

3. What is the theme of this story?

_____

_____

B. Work with a partner. Read the passage aloud. Pay attention to phrasing. Stop after one minute. Fill out the chart.

	Words Read	–	Number of Errors	=	Words Correct Score
First Read		–		=	
Second Read		–		=	

Name _____

Tigris River Valley Boy

The hot sun shone down over the dry valley. Ilulu had been digging for hours and was quite tired. He stopped to take a short rest and looked out over the canals stretching across the valley. Work was coming along well, but there was still much to do before the rainy season arrived. If canals were finished on time, the people of the valley could use the water to grow crops. But if the canals were not finished, the river would flood and wash away the crops.

Answer the questions about the text.

1. How do you know this text is historical fiction?

_____

2. What text feature is included in the text?

_____

3. How does the illustration help you understand the text?

_____

_____

4. How does weather affect people in the Tigris River valley?

_____

_____

Name _____

Read each passage below. Underline the context clues that help you understand each idiom in bold. Then write the meaning of the idiom on the line.

1. My father likes adventure. Mother says that if he isn't exploring, Father is **at sixes and sevens** and he doesn't know what to do with himself!

_____

2. Father **tried his hand** at fishing, but he wasn't much of a success.

_____

3. Father didn't succeed at fishing. He found that he didn't like being on the boat! He must not have **had sea legs**.

_____

4. After **sleeping on it** and giving it a lot of thought, my parents bought a farm in the Middle Colonies.

_____

5. Our life is the best life I can think of—it **takes the cake**! I know my parents made the right choice.

_____

Name _____

A. Read each pair of words. Underline the word that has a final consonant + -*le*, -*el*, or -*al* syllable. Then circle the final syllable. Write the word on the line.

1. able   below   _____

2. glowing   eagle   _____

3. purple   planning   _____

4. valley   squirrel   _____

5. metal   melted   _____

B. Add the suffix to each base word. Write the word on the line. Pay attention to spelling changes.

1. use + able = _____

2. fury + ous = _____

3. ice + y = _____

4. wash + able = _____

5. poison + ous = _____

Name _____

> *Evidence* is details and examples from a text that support a writer's opinion. This student wrote an opinion about whether or not the author gives enough information to help him understand the story's theme.
>
> **Topic sentence** →   In "Warm Enough for Wheat," the author uses what the narrator's family does and says to tell about the theme of making good choices. At the beginning
>
> **Evidence** → of the story, the narrator and her family decide to move to New England. It was cold, and Father didn't like fishing. They were not happy. Then the family decided to move to the Middle Colonies where it was warm. There they could be farmers. I read that this was the right choice for the family. The author
>
> **Concluding statement** → uses what the narrator and her family say and do to help me understand the story's theme about making the right choice.

Write about a story you read. Find text evidence to support your opinion of how the author uses what the characters do and say to share the theme.

Write a topic sentence: _____

_____

Cite evidence from the text: _____

_____

_____

_____

End with a concluding statement: _____

_____

Name _____

A. Read the draft model. Use the questions that follow the draft to help you think about how you can use linking words to connect ideas.

Draft Model

It was the middle of July. Summer is tornado season in Michigan. It was supposed to be a nice day. The sky started getting dark. Tornadoes can form quickly. My brother was surprised at how fast it appeared.

---

1. What linking word might connect the first two ideas?

2. What linking word might show how the third and fourth ideas are different?

3. What linking word might show the relationship between the last two ideas?

B. Now revise the draft by adding linking words to show how ideas are connected.

_____

_____

_____

_____

_____

_____

Name _____

professional	essential	specialist	goal
research	serious	communicated	motivated

Use a word from the box to answer each question. Then use the word in a sentence.

1. **What word might describe someone who does a job for money?**

   _____

2. **What is another word for *aim* or *purpose*?**

   _____

3. **What did the boy do when he wrote a letter to his grandmother?**

   _____

4. **What word might describe someone who is an expert?**

   _____

5. **What word means the opposite of *silly*?**

   _____

6. **What do you need to be in order to take action?**

   _____

7. **What is another word for *necessary*?**

   _____

8. **What is another word for *careful study*?**

   _____

Name _____

Read the selection. Complete the problem and solution graphic organizer.

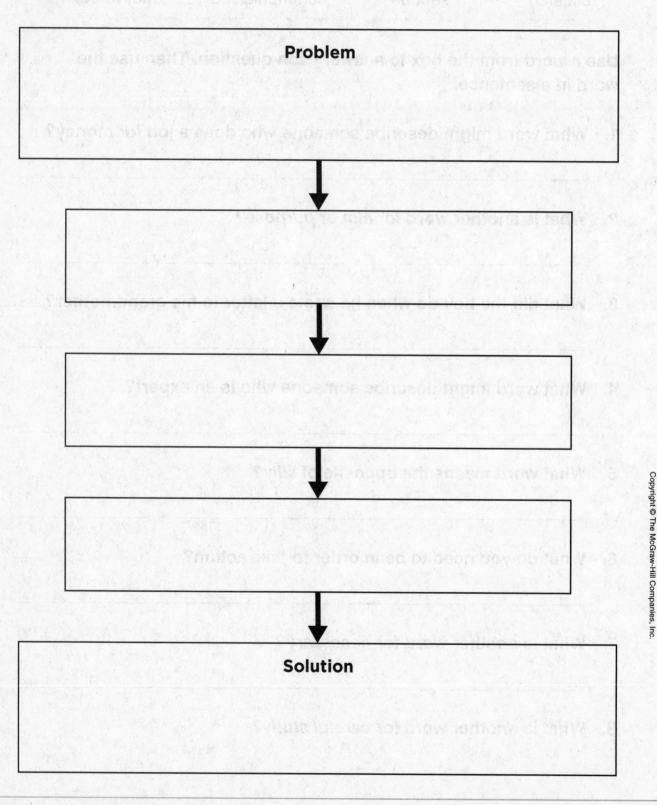

Problem

Solution

Name _____

Read the passage. Use the reread strategy to help you understand the biography.

John Glenn

	Many people admire John Glenn as an American hero. He was
11	a pilot, an astronaut, and a U.S. senator. When he was 77 years
24	old, he became the oldest person ever to fly in space.

35	**Serving His Country**
38	John Glenn was born in Ohio in 1921. When he was 20 years
51	old, World War II broke out. Glenn signed up for the army. Yet he
65	was not called to serve. This was a problem for Glenn. He wanted
78	to serve his country. So Glenn joined the navy. There, he became
90	a pilot. As a pilot, Glenn fought in World War II and the Korean
104	War. Later, he joined the marines.

110	**First Place**
112	John Glenn kept flying after the war. He flew a plane faster
124	than the speed of sound. That's more than 768 miles per hour!
136	He flew the plane all the way across the country. Glenn was the
149	first person to do this. That's why he was picked to be in the U.S.
164	space program. The program is called NASA. At the time, there
175	were only six other astronauts in NASA.
182	Glenn trained for months. On February 20, 1962, Glenn flew
192	in a ship all the way around Earth. He was the first American to
206	orbit Earth.

Name _____

Serving in the Senate

John Glenn had become a famous astronaut. Still, he had another goal. He wanted to be a U.S. senator from Ohio. In 1964 Glenn campaigned for the U.S. Senate. Sadly, he had an accident and hit his head. He was badly injured. He could not keep running for the senate. Yet Glenn did not give up. He tried again. He used his skills as an orator, or public speaker. As a result, he won a senate seat in 1974.

John Glenn served in the senate from 1974 until 1998. During this time, he tried to stop the spread of nuclear weapons. Senator Glenn wrote a law. The law tries to stop people from getting and making nuclear weapons. It also gives rewards to countries that help in this effort.

One More Flight

John Glenn was 77 years old when he left the senate. He was not done serving, though. NASA wanted to find out how space travel affected older people. So they asked Glenn to help. Glenn agreed. In 1998 he flew one final time. He flew around Earth for nine days. He is the oldest person ever to fly in space. John Glenn is a real hero.

John Glenn was the first American to orbit Earth. He served in the U.S. Senate from 1974–1998.

Name _____

A. Reread the passage and answer the questions.

1. Reread paragraph 2 on the first page of the passage. What problem did John Glenn face?

   _____

   _____

2. How did signing up for the navy solve Glenn's problem?

   _____

   _____

3. Reread paragraph 1 on the second page of the passage. What problem did John Glenn face? What was the solution?

   _____

   _____

   _____

B. Work with a partner. Read the passage aloud. Pay attention to accuracy and phrasing. Stop after one minute. Fill out the chart.

	Words Read	–	Number of Errors	=	Words Correct Score
First Read		–		=	
Second Read		–		=	

Name _____

Bessie Coleman

In Chicago, Bessie worked with her brother Walter in a barbershop but still wanted more in life. When her brother John came home after World War I, he teased her, telling her how much better French women were. They had real careers; some even flew airplanes! After hearing this, Bessie decided to become a pilot. As an African American woman, though, she was unable to get a pilot's license in America. With friends' support, she was finally able to enroll in a pilot course in France.

National Aeronautics and Space Administration (NASA)

Bessie Coleman received her pilot's license in France.

Answer the questions about the text.

1. How do you know this text is biography?

_____

_____

2. What text feature is included in the text?

_____

_____

3. How does the text feature help you understand the text?

_____

_____

4. What made Bessie Coleman want to become a pilot?

_____

_____

Name _____

> Greek and Latin root meanings:
>
> *mir* = wonder or amazement   *or* = mouth   *fin* = end
>
> *orb* = circle   *cid* = fall

Use the Greek and Latin roots from the box above to find the meaning of each word in bold below. Write the meaning of the word on the line. Then use each word in a sentence of your own.

1. orbit _____

_____

_____

2. accident _____

_____

_____

3. orator _____

_____

_____

4. admire _____

_____

_____

Name _____

A. Read each sentence. Underline the word with a vowel-team syllable. Then circle the vowel-team syllable.

1. He explained how to get to the lake from his home.

2. She is reading the novel that you gave me.

3. He repeats the sentence so we can write it correctly.

4. Mom had to presoak the shirt to remove all the dirt.

5. I think we forgot to tell him that important detail.

B. Read each sentence. Underline the word with the root *astro, graph, photo,* or *tele*. Write the word on the line and circle the root(s).

1. The astronaut told us about his space mission. _____

2. I checked out a biography on Thomas Edison at the library. _____

3. When I go to college, I want to take a photography class. _____

4. I hope to get a telescope for my birthday. _____

5. We really enjoyed the pictures in this graphic novel. _____

Name _____

Evidence is details and examples from a text that support a writer's ideas. This student wrote about how the author uses signal words to describe John Glenn's problem and how he solved it.

Topic sentence → In "John Glenn," the author used signal words to show how John Glenn solved a problem. At the beginning, John Glenn had a problem. He signed up **Evidence** → for the army, but he was not called to serve. So he joined the navy and became a pilot. The word "so" helps me understand that this is how John solved his problem. Then John wanted to be a U.S. senator, but he lost. As a result, he tried again and won in 1974. The signal words "as a result" help me see that John was able to solve his problem by trying again. The **Concluding statement** → author uses signal words to describe John Glenn's problems and how he solved them.

Write a paragraph about a text you read. Find text evidence to support how the author used signal words to show problem and solution.

Write a topic sentence: _____

_____

Cite evidence from the text: _____

_____

_____

End with a concluding statement: _____

_____

Name _____

A. Read the draft model. Use the questions that follow the draft to help you put the ideas in order.

Draft Model

It is a place to meet friends as well as learn. School is an important part of growing up. That's why it is important to go to school. School teaches valuable skills, like reading.

---

1. Which should be the first sentence in the draft?

2. Which should be the last sentence in the draft?

3. How else should sentences be rearranged to improve the logic of the draft?

B. Now revise the draft by reordering the sentences in a way that makes sense.

_____

_____

_____

_____

_____

_____

_____

Name _____

| illegal | unaware | wildlife | requirement |
| respected | endangered | fascinating | inhabit |

Finish each sentence using the vocabulary word provided.

1. **(inhabit)** There are many types of small animals _____

_____ .

2. **(wildlife)** We took a long hike _____

_____ .

3. **(endangered)** I learned that a certain type of owl _____

_____ .

4. **(illegal)** Driving over the speed limit _____

_____ .

5. **(unaware)** When I left class, _____

_____ .

6. **(requirement)** If I want to get a library card, _____

_____ .

7. **(respected)** My mother had been a teacher for ten years _____

_____ .

8. **(fascinating)** Helping my brother fix his car _____

_____ .

Name _____

Read the selection. Complete the compare and contrast graphic organizer.

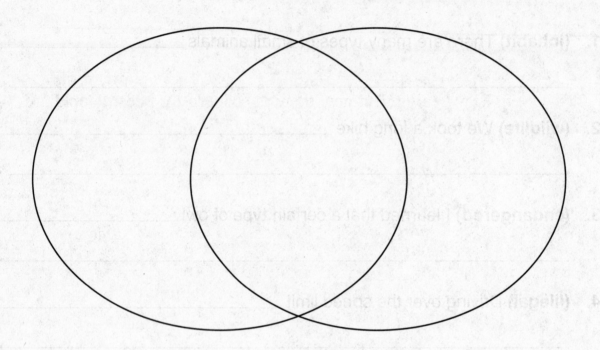

Name _____

Read the passage. Use the reread strategy to help you understand new facts or difficult explanations.

The Disappearance of Bees

13	Take a walk outside in nature. It may not be long before you see bees buzzing around a flower. This is a sight that most people
26	are used to seeing. But now there is concern for bees. People are
39	worried because the number of honey bees has been going down.
49	And no one is sure why.

What Is Happening and Why

55	
60	Studies show that bee colonies in the United States are
70	vanishing. This is a problem that is being called Colony Collapse
81	Disorder. It was first noticed in 2006 by beekeepers. Large groups
92	of bees living together had fewer bees. Since then, nearly
102	one-third of the colonies have gone away.
109	So, what is the cause? The answer is still not clear. Plant sprays
122	may have a role in making the bees sick. Chemicals are often
134	sprayed on plants to keep certain bugs from harming the plants.
145	Newer sprays may be bothering the bees.
152	There are other possible causes. New unknown germs, or tiny
162	living things that can cause disease, may also play a part in
174	getting bees sick. A lack of food and water is also a problem for
188	bees. Too many bees in the hive also adds to the bees' stress.

Name _____

Why We Need Bees

Bees are important to us for many reasons. To start with, they play a big part in growing new plants. They carry a substance called pollen from one part of a plant's flower to another part. The bees can also carry pollen to a new plant. This helps the plant to make seeds. More plants come from the seeds.

Bees carry out the same process, or series of actions, for many plants that farmers grow. A number of these plants, called crops, produce foods that we eat. Apples, carrots, and cherries are a few examples. Fewer bees mean farmers have fewer of these crops.

The bees also affect how many crops there are to buy and sell. Farmers sell the food they grow to stores. The stores sell the food to people. Without bees, buyers would have fewer crops to buy. Sellers would make less money.

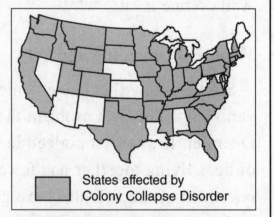

States affected by Colony Collapse Disorder

The map shows states affected by Colony Collapse Disorder, as reported in 2010 by the Congressional Research Service.

Fewer bees would also mean less honey. Honeybees take sweet fluid called nectar from plants. They use this liquid to make honey in their hives. People collect honey. They use it to make foods and drinks sweet. Honey can become scarce, or hard to find, without honeybees.

So the next time you're in your garden, think of the bees. Don't put chemicals on your plants that could harm them. You will be happy you did.

Name _____

A. Reread the passage and answer the questions.

1. What do the things mentioned in paragraphs 3–4 have in common?

_____

_____

2. How are the things mentioned in paragraphs 3–4 different from one another?

_____

_____

_____

3. Compare and contrast pollen and nectar in paragraphs 5 and 8. How are they similar and different?

_____

_____

_____

B. Work with a partner. Read the passage aloud. Pay attention to phrasing. Stop after one minute. Fill out the chart.

	Words Read	–	Number of Errors	=	Words Correct Score
First Read		–		=	
Second Read		–		=	

Name _____

What Good Are Mosquitoes?

Some people think mosquitoes are not very helpful animals. After all, most of us know mosquitoes because of their itching bite. But mosquitoes are an important part of the food chain. For example, dragonflies rely on mosquitoes to eat. Without a large mosquito population, dragonflies could not survive. If the number of dragonflies drops enough, animals that depend on dragonflies might not survive.

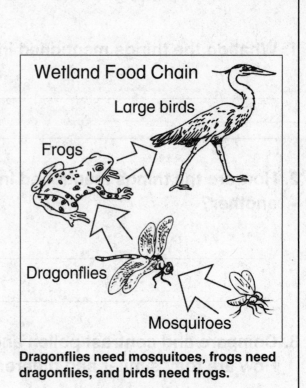

Wetland Food Chain

Large birds

Frogs

Dragonflies

Mosquitoes

Dragonflies need mosquitoes, frogs need dragonflies, and birds need frogs.

Answer the questions about the text.

1. How do you know this text is expository text?

_____

2. What text feature is included in the text?

_____

3. How does the text feature help you understand the topic?

_____

4. Why are mosquitoes important?

_____

Name _____

Read the sentences below. Underline the context clues that help you understand the meaning of each word in bold. Then write the meaning of the word in bold on the line.

1. Now there is **concern** for bees. People are worried because the number of honeybees has been going down. And no one is sure why.

   _____

2. Studies show that bee **colonies** in the United States are vanishing. This is a problem that is being called Colony Collapse Disorder. It was first noticed in 2006 by beekeepers. Large groups of bees living together had fewer bees.

   _____

3. New unknown **germs**, or tiny living things that can cause disease, may also play a part in getting bees sick. A lack of food and water is also a problem for bees.

   _____

4. Bees carry out the same **process**, or series of actions, for many plants that farmers grow.

   _____

5. Honeybees take sweet **fluid** called nectar from plants. They use this liquid to make honey in their hives.

   _____

Name _____

A. Read each sentence. Underline the word with an *r*-controlled vowel syllable. Write the word on the line. Then circle the *r*-controlled vowel syllable.

1. She put the canned fruit in the cool cellar. _____

2. The author read from his new book. _____

3. I hope to go to the skating rink later. _____

4. My dad is helping his friend restore an old truck. _____

5. The circus was in town last week. _____

B. Read the words with the Latin suffixes *-able* and *-ment* in the box. Match a word from the box to each meaning below. Write the word on the line. Not all words will be used.

movement	usable	excitement	argument
adorable	enjoyable	agreeable	encouragement

1. an act of arguing _____

2. able to be used _____

3. an act of moving _____

4. able to be adored _____

5. an act of encouraging _____

6. able to be enjoyed _____

Name _____

Evidence is details and examples from a text that support a writer's ideas. This student wrote about how the author compares and contrasts information to explain a topic.

Topic sentence →   In "The Disappearance of Bees," the author compares and contrasts pollen and nectar to explain why bees are important. I read that bees take pollen

Evidence → from one part of a plant's flower to another. Pollen helps plants make seeds. Bees take nectar from plants back to their hives. People collect honey. Both pollen and nectar come from plants. The author

Concluding statement → compares and contrasts pollen and nectar to show how important bees are to plants and people.

Write a paragraph about a text you read. Find text evidence to show how the author compares and contrasts information to explain a topic.

Write a topic sentence: _____

_____

Cite evidence from the text: _____

_____

_____

_____

_____

End with a concluding statement: _____

_____

Name _____

A. Read the draft model. Use the questions that follow the draft to help you think about how you can add a strong conclusion that retells the main idea.

Draft Model

I did not like pigs. I thought that pigs were dirty. I didn't think they were smart. Then I learned pigs are some of the smartest animals on the planet. Pigs can even be kept as pets.

---

1. What is the main idea?

2. What did the narrator learn about pigs being dirty?

3. What did the narrator learn about pigs being smart?

4. What conclusion could be added to retell the main idea?

B. Now revise the draft by adding a strong conclusion that retells the main idea.

_____

_____

_____

_____

_____

_____

Name _____

| entertainment | ridiculous | humorous | slithered |

Use a word from the box to answer each question. Then use the word in a sentence.

1. What does a performer provide? _____

_____

_____

2. What is another word for *funny*? _____

_____

_____

3. What did the snake do as it moved through the grass? _____

_____

_____

4. What word might describe someone who is acting very silly? _____

_____

_____

Name _____

Read the selection. Complete the point of view graphic organizer.

Details

↓

Point of View

Name _____

Read the poem. Check your understanding by asking yourself how the narrator thinks or feels.

Aliens!

	While waiting in the car for Mom,
7	Dad says, sounding very profound,
12	"I'm afraid I have to drop a bomb:
20	there are *aliens* around.
24	We didn't want to tell you boys,
31	we thought it might just freak you out.
39	I need you to stay calm and keep your poise
49	while I tell you what this is about.
57	We taught you not to fear the new.
65	We told you that the world was strange,
73	but what we didn't say to you
80	is that we are one end of the range
89	of things that folks don't understand.
95	If others knew, they'd make a fuss.
102	And though our lives are pretty bland,
109	the fact is that the aliens are *us*!"
117	Mom opened her door and got inside.
124	I was shocked as we flew into the sky.
133	But Mom was clever enough to say,
140	"Did something go down while I was away?"

Name _____

A. Reread the passage and answer the questions.

1. What is this poem about?

_____

_____

_____

2. What is the narrator's point of view in the poem?

_____

_____

_____

3. What clues in the poem tell you the narrator's point of view?

_____

_____

B. Work with a partner. Read the passage aloud. Pay attention to phrasing and expression. Stop after one minute. Fill out the chart.

	Words Read	−	Number of Errors	=	Words Correct Score
First Read		−		=	
Second Read		−		=	

Name _____

The Snowman

We made his eyes out of pudding cups,
    his mouth from pizza crust.
His mustache was tortilla chips
    we'd pounded into dust.

In his right hand we stuck a broken stick
    topped by a tuna tin.
His left hand held the head that wore
    a grim leftover grin.

Answer the questions about the poem.

1. How many stanzas does this poem have? How many lines does each stanza have?

_____

2. Which lines in the first stanza rhyme?

_____

3. What does the poem tell a story about?

_____

4. What does the speaker think of the snowman?

_____

_____

_____

Name _____

Read the lines of the narrative poem below. Then answer the questions.

Aliens!

While waiting in the car for Mom,
Dad says, sounding very profound,
"I'm afraid I have to drop a bomb:
there are aliens around.

We didn't want to tell you boys,
we thought it might just freak you out.
I need you to stay calm and keep your poise
while I tell you what this is about.

---

1. Find two examples of rhyme in the poem. Write them on the line.

_____

2. How can you pick out the rhythm in the poem?

_____

3. Write another stanza for this poem that includes rhythm and rhyme.

_____

_____

_____

_____

Name _____

**Read each passage. Write the idiom in the passage on the line.
Then write the meaning of the idiom.**

1. I'm afraid I have to drop a bomb:
there are *aliens* around.

_____

_____

2. We didn't want to tell you boys,
we thought it might just freak you out.

_____

_____

3. But Mom was clever enough to say,
"Did something go down while I was away?"

_____

_____

Name _____

A. Read the words with the suffixes -less, -ful, and -ly in the word box. Match each word to the correct meaning below. Write the word on the line. Not all words will be used.

wisely	hopeful	finally	careless
endless	adorable	argument	pitiful

1. full of pity _____

2. in a final way _____

3. without care _____

4. in a wise way _____

5. without end _____

6. full of hope _____

B. Read each sentence below. Choose the correct word from the word box to complete each sentence. Write the word on the line. Not all the words will be used. Use a dictionary to check your answers.

thorough	your	scissors	through
sissors	journey	you're	weather
gourney	perswade	persuade	minute

1. Mom found _____ coat under the bed.

2. We will need _____ for this art project.

3. We did a _____ job cleaning the kitchen.

4. The speaker told us about her exciting _____ to India.

5. An advertisement tries to _____ you to buy something.

6. The clock ticked down to the final _____ of the game.

Name _____

Evidence is details and examples from a text that support a writer's ideas. The student who wrote the paragraph below found text evidence that shows how the author uses details to show the narrator's point of view about some surprising news.

Topic sentence → In "Aliens!," the author uses details to tell how the narrator learned about who he really is. In this poem, the narrator is a young boy. Dad starts to tell

Evidence → him the truth about his family. The narrator says that Dad is profound and serious. Dad explains that the brothers should stay calm. The narrator at the end tells us that everyone in their family is an alien as their car takes off into space. The author uses

Concluding statement → details about how Dad breaks the news that they are aliens to show that he was shocked and surprised at the end of the poem.

Write about a poem you have read. Find text evidence to show how the author uses what the narrator thinks to share the narrator's point of view.

Write a topic sentence: _____

_____

Cite evidence from the text: _____

_____

_____

_____

End with a concluding statement: _____

_____

Name _____

A. Read the draft model. Use the questions that follow the draft to help you think about what precise words you can add.

Draft Model

Clowns make me laugh. I like going to the circus. It is funny when lots of clowns get out of a car. One clown is always in the park. He makes balloon animals for all the kids.

---

1. What precise words could be used to help make the draft model clearer for the reader?

2. What precise words would help readers visualize the clowns, the car, and the park?

3. What adjectives could be used to describe the balloon animals?

B. Now revise the draft by adding precise words to help make the draft model more interesting to read.

_____

_____

_____

_____

_____

_____

_____